# *Hands and Heart Together*

Daily Meditations for Caregivers

*BOOKS BY PATRICIA HOOLIHAN*

*Hands and Heart Together: Daily Meditations for Caregivers* (Holy Cow! Press, 2021)

*Storm Prayers: Retrieving and Reimagining Matters of the Soul* (North Star Press, 2014)

*Launching Your Teen into Adulthood: Parenting Through the Transition* (Search Institute Press, 2009)

*A Moment's Peace for Parents of Teens – 365 Rejuvenating Reflections* (Search Institute Press, 2007)

*Teen Girls Only! Daily Thoughts for Teenage Girls* (Holy Cow! Press, 2001)

*Small Miracles: Daily Meditations for Mothers in Recovery* (Bantam, 1992)

*Today's Gift: Meditations for Families*, co-author, (Hazelden, 1985)

*Stress and Recovery* (Hazelden, 1984)

# *Hands and Heart Together*

Daily Meditations for Caregivers

by

Patricia Hoolihan

Holy Cow! Press • 2021 • Duluth, Minnesota

Author photograph by Judy Griesedieck.

Cover art by Susan Armington.

Cover and book design by Marlene Wisuri,
Dovetailed Press, LLC.

Printed and bound in the United States of America.

ISBN 978-1513645643

First printing, Winter, 2021

10 9 8 7 6 5 4 3 2 1

Holy Cow! Press projects are funded in part by grant awards from the Ben and Jeanne Overman Charitable Trust, the Elmer L. and Eleanor J. Andersen Foundation, the Lenfestey Family Foundation, Schwegman Lundberg & Woessner, P.A., and by gifts from generous individual donors. We are grateful to Springboard for the Arts for their support as our fiscal sponsor.

Holy Cow! Press books are distributed to the trade by Consortium Book Sales & Distribution, c/o Ingram Publisher Services, Inc., 210 American Drive, Jackson, TN 38301.

For inquiries, please write to: Holy Cow! Press, Post Office Box 3170, Mount Royal Station, Duluth, MN 55803.

Visit www.holycowpress.org.

## *Acknowledgments/Gratitudes*

The first round of grateful thanks goes to Jim Perlman of Holy Cow! Press who said yes when this book was just a fledgling and whose encouragement all along the way helped give it wings. Deep thanks to Susan Armington for our gorgeous cover art, to Marlene Wisuri for the wonderful layout and design of the cover and all pages, and to Christine Stevens whose editorial eye sharpened many a page.

The next round of thanks goes out to a huge group of family members and friends, too many to name, who contributed your stories, your wide-ranging experiences, your tears and tender moments, and your favorite inspirational quotes. This book is enriched by all of you, and I am deeply indebted to your generosity and shared wisdom.

I am grateful for the contributions of all my siblings to the caregiving of our parents, aunts, and uncle. I am especially grateful to my sister Jane, nurse and caregiver extraordinaire, for her teamwork and how she often led the way as we cared for our parents—especially Mom in her last years. A special shoutout to our husbands, who helped out and held us up through the journey, especially those hours in the ER.

Eternal gratitude to my parents, aunts, and uncle for the way they shared the journey of their last years with me; I am forever touched and deepened by what I learned from them.

A huge round of thank yous to the wise sages, poets, and writers whose words I have used here. I owe a huge debt of gratitude to all of you, for how your words inspired me and for how your words shine a special light into these meditations. I deeply appreciate every opening quote in this book. I send out a special thanks to those writers who appear on these pages multiple times: Tove Pettersen (*Conceptions of Care: Altruism, Feminism, and Mature Care*), Kirsten DeLeo (*Present Through the End–A Caring Companion's Guide for Accompanying the Dying*), Atul Gawande (*Being Mortal: Medicine and What Matters in the End*), Jane Gross (*A Bittersweet Season: Caring for Our Aging Parents and Ourselves*), Mark Nepo (*The Book of Awakening*), Caroline Johnson (*The Caregiver*), Richard Wagamese (*Embers: One Ojibway's Meditations*), and Brene Brown (*The Power of Vulnerability* and *The Gifts of Imperfection*). The beautiful and inspiring words of poets also grace these pages: endless thanks to Mary Oliver (may she rest in peace), rupi kaur, and many others. A special thanks for song lyrics that bring music and melody to this process of caregiving, and likewise grace these meditations.

Last but not least, waves of gratitude for my always encouraging husband, my amazing adult children and son-in-law who remind me every day how to be a passionate human being. I am so grateful for the beneficent gift of grandchildren in my life who may have taken me away from my writing at times but always found a way to inspire it—since what connects the rivers between caregiving and grandparenting and everything in between is the current of love.

This book is dedicated to caregivers everywhere—past, present, and future.

# *Preface*

I will always remember crossing the threshold of the hospital room my aunt was lying in; the stroke rendered her unable to drink water and made her speech difficult to understand. I had just driven 200 miles in response to the exhaustion I heard in my parents' voices. They and my other aunt and uncle—all my father's siblings, all in their 80s—had been attending to my aunt around-the-clock since her stroke. Decades earlier, this group had come to my bedside during a near-death medical emergency; their presence brought me enormous comfort and eased my fears.

Now it was my turn to show up at a loved one's bedside. My initial feeling was that I didn't really know what I was doing or what I had to offer; I felt awkward, overwhelmed. I would bet that many of you who pick up this book can relate to those feelings. I spent the next few hours watching how they all cared for her, talked to her, took turns, worked with the nurses. The depth and simplicity of their shared caring opened my heart in unexpected ways. My aunt herself, in her weakened state, had ways of communicating her needs and desires. What I learned in this initial round of caregiving was the importance of listening and paying attention, and the utter difference made by kind and simple gestures. Even on that first evening, as my solo shift in the hospital was at hand, after a few words of encouragement from my uncle before he headed out the door, my confidence had grown. When my aunt raised her hand out of semi-sleep, I rose and held it. She clasped my hand tight. A simple gesture: deeply moving moment for me, comfort for her.

A deep respect settled in me for what was happening among this group of loved ones, as it had decades earlier when I was so vulnerable. As I entered their world of caregiving, I felt immersed in a deeply meaningful, even sacred, mystery. Who we all were to each other, how we took turns shoring each other up, and how we all felt connected by our concern for her vulnerability touched and shaped me at deep levels.

There have been many rounds of caregiving since then, as each one of that group at my aunt's bedside at some point became the most vulnerable one. As there were fewer of them, it became more important for me and my generation to step into this caregiver role. The last survivors of this group were my father and mother—my mother outliving him by four years. Through it all, I have learned that caregiving requires both hands-on practical assistance and an ability to see and listen with one's heart: thus, the title of this book is *Hands and Heart Together*. The exhaustion that I heard in my parents' voice that day years ago, I have lived in my own bones. The lessons of love in action that I observed then, I have had many opportunities to practice over the years; I am grateful for the role models I had.

Beyond that, I am not trained in any way that might be obvious for a caregiver. I am not a nurse or a doctor. Nor am I a psychologist or a minister, although I do have a daily prayer/meditation/writing practice. For me, and for many others, a need arose in a loved one (over the years multiple loved ones) for hands-on and heartfelt care, and I felt called to respond. Whether you are caring for a spouse, a parent, a sibling, extended family member, or a good friend, you have most likely felt called to respond to that loved one's needs. Once on that path, I came to realize that many days were hard and rugged and exhausting. Every spiritual and psychological tool I knew of was needed to stay on the path.

For years, I have been a faithful reader of several daily meditation books; they help me pay attention to the deeper levels at work in my days. As a caregiver, however, I longed for a daily reflection that was more specific to the challenges of caregiving. I longed for a meaningful reminder of my worth in this role. The beauty of the daily meditation book is that it travels well and can be read in a short amount of time—a commodity hard to come by for most caregivers. Yet, the words carry a reader into a few centered moments—and those moments shed light on all that your day holds. This book of daily reflections for caregivers has lived inside of me for a long time; it is the book I wish I had had then.

We all come to caregiving in different ways, and each situation has its own special challenges. Yet, what seems to be true for every caregiver is that they see a need and step in to fulfill that need. For those of you who live with your loved one, your experience is even more intense than for the rest of us: I salute your courage and very hands-on care. Caregiving in any way entails wrestling with a few soul-searching questions: 1) What kind of human being do I want to be? 2) Who has this loved one been to me, and what am I willing and able to give in return? 3) How would I want to be cared for and by whom if I were to be the most vulnerable one?

Each of us answers these questions in our own way. These meditations provide entry points for every reader to circle back to the core of who they are and why they have chosen this meaningful path; they offer a daily reminder and exploration of these elemental questions. May this book provide you, the reader, with inspiration when you need it and comfort when you seek it. May it every day remind you that you are not alone. Far from it, there are over 43 million family caregivers in the United States, according to AARP. These readings provide gentle guidance to honor both the burdens and beautiful gifts of this journey—one day at a time. My experiences, mistakes, regrets, as well as those of many people I have talked to and who have shared this path, infuse these pages and will hopefully inspire a deep wisdom in your caregiving.

The reflections in this book are intended to help sustain and inspire caregivers, yet they are useful for anyone who is part of the support team for a caregiver. Many caregivers say they couldn't have done it if they hadn't had a supportive spouse or friend. Whether you are a primary or secondary caregiver or the one who supports the caregiver, your role matters and makes a difference.

Feel free to adapt the daily focus of these meditations to your specific needs; although I have covered many different aspects of caregiving, each situation carries its own complexities. Take what works for you here and leave the rest. The meditations are designed to be read daily, but if a particular day's reading isn't helpful, I encourage you to flip through the pages and find one that resonates. The arrival of COVID-19 has had a huge impact on caregiving, and since it arrived near the end of my writing, there are a few meditations which address it. Some meditations focus on holidays, the dates of which change from year to year. They are set up for 2021, so in subsequent years you may need to look ahead or behind in the book for that specific holiday's reading.

The caregiving path is not for the faint of heart. But it is filled with gentle and surprising gifts. This daily reflection book is meant to be a tool to help sustain you, to help you continue to discern where and when to draw boundaries, and most of all to help you stay clear and wholehearted about this journey you are on with a loved one. May these meditations light the way as you, with hands and heart together, live into your own answers. Caregiving is a journey that won't last forever (though sometimes it feels like it), yet its gifts will shed light upon you for the rest of your life.

Patricia Hoolihan
August 2020

# January

## *January 1*

***"O Sunlight! The most precious gold to be found on Earth."***

—Roman Payne

As we collectively enter a new year, our hearts and minds have a clear opportunity to open to the simple and always-available blessings of the earth and of light. No matter what is going on around us, the sun rises every morning. It dispels the darkness of the night, it erases the shadows of half-light, and it makes visible what has been rendered—for the hours of the night—invisible. The sunrise and the sun's movement across our landscape are daily visual metaphors for the deeper process of trusting that the darkness on our trail will at some point find the clarity of light.

The nourishment of the earth becomes visible in this light. Even in stark winter climates, the beauty can be dramatic. Beauty—the rhythms at work in nature, birdsong, trees in all seasons—nourishes our tired hearts.

Our caregiving hearts can always find blessings in these simple and tangible forms of beauty.

*As I enter a new year as a caregiver, I will reach for nourishment from the earth and from the simple clarity bestowed by sunlight.*

## *January 2*

***"Love begins by taking care of the closest ones—the ones at home."***

—Mother Teresa

These words are from a world-renowned and time-honored sage and saint. Although she traveled far from her own home to enter different worlds of need, in her wisdom she reminds all of us that genuine love begins with how we treat those who have been closest to us. In our lives, we may have traveled away from the loved one we are now caring for, yet there has always been a thread of continuity, a thread that sews together our past and our present, a thread that holds the power to heal and mend.

There is little if any glamour on this path of caregiving, but the love at its core is a deep river that will carry you to the sea. On the way, the rocks embedded on the riverbanks will become touchstones you walk upon, finger for their strength, and carry in your pockets for their silent promise of answers.

Love is my teacher, and it is teaching me in ways I cannot always see. This richness is right here, close to home.

## *January 3*

***"At heart, hospitality is helping across a threshold."***

—Ivan Illich

When I look back upon the months I cared for my mother before her death, I realize that in many small ways I was helping her to cross that threshold toward leaving this world. The few times she talked about it and I listened were one of the ways I was a quiet and encouraging part of her journey. The cups of tea we shared were simple moments of sharing time—something we both knew was limited.

Some days I helped with small items on the list: pick up Gatorade for her, help with a load of laundry, sweep the floor where she spilled the sugar. It was easy to feel that I wasn't doing much or that I wasn't doing enough. Perhaps it is easier to see from a distance how those small gestures brought her comfort and how the simple moments shared kept her company. They provided hospitality, warmth, and care, and softened the hard glint of her days of physical pain and anxiety.

*Today I will honor the sacredness of my small, simple gestures that are part of a larger picture of caring hospitality.*

## *January 4*

***"My goal in life is to not only survive, but to thrive; and to do so with some passion, some humor, and some style."***

—Maya Angelou

There is no doubt about the fact that caregiving is very demanding. I remember days when I felt keenly aware that what I was experiencing—the almost daily onslaught of needs coming at me—was the hardest thing I had ever gone through. Admittedly, there were only some days that felt like that. Many days, humor helped. Sometimes a small laugh between my mother and me lightened up everything. Near the end, there were days when she rhymed her words. She might have the "glue," meaning flu. She needed to brush her "feet," meaning teeth. We both laughed. I can laugh at the silliness of it years after she passed away.

Those small moments of humor are to be celebrated. For that moment, you are two (or more) people enjoying the gift of shared laughter, even if it's just a quiet chuckle.

*When humor makes its appearance, I will let it lighten my heart and not hurry through the moment. Sharing such moments with my loved one lightens both of our hearts in healing ways.*

## *January 5*

***"This time, like all times, is a very good one, if we but know what to do with it."***

—Ralph Waldo Emerson

The moments we spend with a loved one, especially one who is aging or ailing or struggling in other ways, are precious. Even though we have a subliminal awareness of limited time, it is often hard to hold onto the heightened sense of meaning that is inherent in that term. Time itself is the gift; time shared is its exponential value, time spent in each other's company. Whether it's a half hour of shared tea time or an afternoon of small chores and visiting, time is the gift of the day.

Yes, there are always other needs and schedules pulling at most of us. Rarely is providing care for this special person our only responsibility. But rather than seeing the list of to-dos, we can let that go for a time and sink deeply into the sharing of time, the giving of care as best we can for today.

*Today, hard as it may be at the edges, is a good day. I will embrace it fully, especially simple time spent with my loved one.*

## *January 6*

***"Día de los Reyes" is a significant holiday celebration across Latin America. Known formally as the Feast of the Epiphany, "Día de los Reyes" commemorates the visit of the three kings or the Magi to Baby Jesus, thereby representing Christ's physical revelation to the gentiles."***

—The Yucatan Times

January 6 is a special feast day, especially for Latin Americans. It is also known as Epiphany and as the 12th day of Christmas. This day celebrates the visitation of the three Magi kings to baby Jesus. The word magi comes from the same root word that informs the word magic. These three magi were most likely persons of high learning and well-acquainted with the study of the stars. They were following a star; the sky led them to Bethlehem. It was not an easy journey, but they followed the star and brought with them gifts of gold, frankincense and myrrh.

There is meaning to be found in all of this, no matter our religious or ethnic background. It is about celebrating the birth of a child, about watching and paying attention to the stars in the sky, and about simple gifts that connect the givers and the receivers. It is about traditions that live on because they celebrate birth and death and community, so elemental to all of humanity.

*We caregivers can honor "Dia de los Reyes Magos" in our own way by honoring the gifts of our journey, both received and given, and by reaching skyward for the perception and insight promised by the word epiphany.*

## *January 7*

***"Many of our ancestors crossed oceans and barriers to seek fluency in a new world for the generations to come. And many of them, at some point, were caregivers."***

—Patricia Hoolihan. *journal*

Fluency implies and is defined by the words flowing, graceful, and adaptable. These are qualities that can be hard to find in days of caregiving with its many changes and challenges. Yet we can seek fluency in any day. The ocean has its many moods, its wide open and vast expanses of water and sky, its waves that crest and then fall, its music as it rushes to shore and then recedes, making lyrical sounds among the tiny grains of sand and rock. Caregiving embraces many moods and the rise and fall of many a wave. Its particular music becomes a background melody for our day-to-day lives.

As we seek such fluency, we can also look for and invoke the protection of ancestors. Many of our ancestors also lived through difficult times. Many of our ancestors knew intimately the importance of caring for one another.

*As the new year begins, may I be blessed with a gracefulness like moving waters and by the continuous thread of care my ancestors have bestowed to me across time.*

## *January 8*

**"Please remember it is what you are that heals, not what you know."**

—Carl Jung

When you are caring for someone who is losing strength in any way, there is no magic ingredient you are required to manufacture to fix it, nor are there any magic solutions. The strength you bring and that lives within you is enough. Who you are, not what you know nor what solutions you may or may not be able to effect, is what really matters. Healing qualities are embedded in genuine care, in gentle gestures, and in the message you reveal by simply showing up.

Listening to your loved one, accepting them where they are at, being there—these are the simple and direct ways to bring healing into a difficult time or situation. Listening with your heart and paying attention to your flashes of intuition can guide you through the day-to-day needs better than anything else.

*I am being given many opportunities to listen deeply and respond with my heart and intuition. That is all I need to do for today.*

## *January 9*

**"Sleep that knits up the ravelled sleeve of care."**

—Shakespeare

Is your ability to care flagging? Do you feel at your wit's end, as if this chosen role is more than you can really do? You would not be the only caregiver in the world who has brushed up against such feelings. It is incredibly demanding, especially in a period where there are several things that go wrong.

It is helpful to remember that not all weeks are like that. Usually such feelings are a red flag that you need a break, that you are tired. Very often a simple solution is a good night's rest or perhaps a nap. Certainly if you have had a few rugged days, find a way to carve out time to sleep. Sleep, as Shakespeare so eloquently says, knits up the wear and tear of crises, which unravel us all. Exhaustion happens, but it is not a healthy place to give care from for any extended time. Get through what needs to be taken care of, and then sleep. Rest. It truly does rejuvenate you for whatever is ahead.

*When exhaustion comes upon me, in its clever disguises, I will find a way to recognize it and carve out the time to rest and refresh. Balancing rest with caregiving is an important aspect of this ongoing journey.*

## *January 10*

***"To love is to accept a soul entirely, not wishing that the person was otherwise, nor hoping for change, nor clinging to some ideal past."***

—Richelle E. Goodrich, *Smile Anyway*

At its root, caregiving is a choice to love, to love through a difficult and challenging time or situation. There is no other or better reason to do it. In that way, it is a path for practicing love and acceptance for who he or she is today, who our loved has become. We may wish things were different, but ultimately this is a life path that demands acceptance every day. Hoping for change or clinging to some version of the past are akin to walking into a wall over and over again.

Acceptance with love means to accept and honor who your loved one is today—messy? Forgetful? Short-tempered? Anxious? Needy? In spite of more difficult traits, is there some part of this person that is more open to you than ever before? Funnier than ever? More accepting of his or her own state? Sometimes on a cloudy day, the occasional rays that break forth from small openings can bring one alive with such fleeting beauty. Acceptance allows the heart to open to those surprising moments in the midst of the difficult ones.

*Rather than wishing things were different today, I will embrace my loved one as he or she is and look for the light shining through a break in the clouds.*

## *January 11*

**"Sometimes a person needs a story more than food to stay alive. . . . This is how people care for each other."**

—Barry Lopez from *Crow and Weasel*

Storytelling allows you and your loved one to travel while sitting still: travel through laughter or shared memory to a distant place or a moment that is full of light. Maybe you have a story to tell your loved one that is based in a shared memory. Perhaps it's a story of something in your day that made you laugh or smile or pause. The telling of a story can be a gift in and of itself. All it requires is a bit of inspiration and the willingness to take the time to enter story land.

We all have stories to tell—stories that have lived inside us for a long time or stories that arise in the course of day-to-day living. One day the snowfall reminded me of a time when I was ten and we had a snow day from school. Telling the story to my mother of going out sledding and coming in for hot chocolate and her homemade rolls made us both smile. Its memory warmed our time together and warmed the cold edges of that particular day.

*When the day triggers the memory of a story, I will take time to share it and enjoy it with my loved one. This is an important way we care for each other.*

## *January 12*

**"As our time winds down, we all seek comfort in simple pleasures—companionship, everyday routines, the taste of good food, the warmth of sunlight on our faces."**

—Atul Gawande

As a caregiver, you are probably already highly tuned to the routines that are important to your loved one. But it never hurts to ask what a simple pleasure would be today or tomorrow. They sometimes change. When my father was near the end, he loved snacking on small pretzels, and he loved oatmeal with brown sugar. For my mother, it was small nibble-size cookies and hot tea.

No matter what pain or hardship might have been passing through the day, the simple pleasure of a favorite food, especially when shared, always brought relief to the room. I didn't always feel like I was doing much when I sat at the table with my mom, but looking back, those are some of my favorite times with her. Just being with her, sipping our favorite tea and munching on those small cookies that we both loved, sharing companionable small talk—it was all that mattered in those expansive moments. And it was more than enough to fill both of our hearts.

*Facilitating my loved one's simple pleasures and sharing them is all I need to do today. It is more than enough.*

## *January 13*

***"I have loved best***
***how the flowers rise***
***and open, how***
***the pink lungs of their bodies***
***. . . stand there shining."***

—Mary Oliver

No one has appreciated the arrival of flowers more than my mother or my wonderful aunts in their days when they were homebound or in their assisted living apartments. All had been gardeners and had at one time owned homes where the perennials gave them annual and seasonal pleasure. All I had to do was arrive with a bundle of color in my arms, and the day itself grew brighter.

And at the end of my visit, as I said goodbye for that day, I knew my flowers would continue to open, to shine their color and hopeful energy into the days ahead. Of course, they didn't last forever, but their fleetingness never detracted from the joy given and received. The scent of an aromatic rose or a pastel freesia filled the room—we all breathed deeply their scents of beauty.

*The simple gift of flowers is always a gift of beauty and hope, when I have the time and am able.*

## *January 14*

**"When written in Chinese, the word crisis has two characters. One represents danger, the other opportunity."**

—John Fitzgerald Kennedy

Crises are a part of the aging and ailing process. Body parts break down, vulnerabilities lead to accidents, weak immune systems can't fight common colds or flus. I would be hard-pressed to say that a crisis is ever a good thing because, after all, crises represent trouble and further problems. When my phone rang at 5:00 a.m. and I saw it was from my sister, I knew before I ever picked up that something had gone wrong with Mom during the night. My adrenaline would kick in immediately. There were many such phone calls, jarring me from sleep or from other plans or from an ordinary day.

Yet every crisis was handled. Every crisis gave my sister and I and other family members a chance to work together. Often, a crisis presented an opportunity for a conversation that would not have happened otherwise. Sometimes a crisis pushed us toward the next necessary decision. And occasionally the crisis gave my mother a chance to let us know how much she appreciated being able to count on us when things went awry. It did hearken back to all the times she took care of me and my siblings when we were young and sick.

*Rather than wishing they wouldn't happen, I can accept that some crises are a normal part of this journey. I can be open to the opportunity that exists at the outside edges of the possible dangers.*

## *January 15*

**"Alone we can do so little; together we can do so much."**

—Helen Keller

If you are lucky, you have another family member/friend or more helping you with the care you are giving a loved one. If you are the sole family/friend caregiver, having a support team of some sort is so important for long-term sanity. Hopefully, you have a supportive partner or a couple of good friends who understand what you are going through, even if they are not in a position to help you with the caregiving itself.

Often there are professionals who are part of the team. Awareness of and appreciation for your team is an important part of this journey. It's so easy to get caught up in the daily demands and needs, but so important to take time to reach out to your support people when you need some extra shoring up. Gratitude for their being there is always appreciated and helps build the team synergy that will carry you through.

*It doesn't take much time, only a conscious intention, to acknowledge and thank those who are helping me on this journey. I couldn't do it alone.*

## *January 16*

***"I have just three things to teach: simplicity, patience, compassion. These are your greatest treasures."***

—Lao Tzu

This ancient Chinese philosopher and sage speaks across the centuries a truth that resonates in today's world, especially for those of us involved in caregiving. Simplicity. Often the needs of one whose health is declining are simpler than we realize. Yes, there are the medical complications which are important to address. But beyond that, the needs are often simple and simply met: a hand to hold, a listening ear, a well-timed phone call, time shared.

Compassion is the cornerstone here. Compassion and empathy for what your loved one is going through, even when you don't understand it, is the key to providing a healthy and loving touchstone. Patience with the small irritations is the embodiment of compassion.

*My path today is one of connecting with myself as caregiver and with my loved one—through simple gestures, a patient attitude, and a deep compassion.*

## *January 17*

**"Even though we had a great visit, I still left tired. It's the weight of loss and impending loss, all woven together."**

—Patricia Hoolihan, *journal*

The above entry is from my journal during my days of caregiving my mother. Some days I tried to fight that sense of tiredness, or some days it didn't make sense to me. But it truly does make sense that being in the presence of loss—the loss of who your loved one used to be or the awareness that their failing health means limited time left to share—has a palpable impact.

Loss is an inextricable part of this journey. And there are times when that loss will feel heavy. It helps to understand that—to give yourself full permission to be compassionate toward yourself on those days. Caregiving is not an easy road. If there is someone you can talk to who will understand your challenges and can give you the needed encouragement, then tired days are the days to reach toward such a friend. Nurture yourself in gentle ways to soften the hard and tired edges of loss.

*By acknowledging loss as part of the journey, I can find a healthy way to comfort myself when loss rolls through me.*

## *January 18*

***"Ice cream is the perfect buffer, because you can do things in a somewhat lighthearted way. . . . I think when you combine caring, and eating wonderful food, it's a very powerful combination."***

—Jerry Greenfield

In my mother's last months, we discovered that a small caramel sundae was something she really enjoyed. And I mean enjoyed, almost swooned over. Great attention was paid to each small bite. At first she fed herself, and at some point I was delivering the caramel swirled soft ice cream to her by the spoonful. Either way, the pleasure she took in its sensuous deliciousness was clear. All else stopped. The progression of time was momentarily suspended. For a few moments, the pain in her body subsided, and her worries went away.

I admit it. I enjoyed them also. Together we soaked up the pleasure. And years later, if I am missing her, I stop and buy a caramel soft ice cream sundae and savor it. I savor the memory of sharing time with her and of finding a small way to clearly lift her spirits.

*I will share a lighthearted treat with*
*my loved one—if not today, then soon.*

## *January 19*

***"It's hard to practice compassion when we're struggling with our authenticity or when our own worthiness is off-balance."***

—Brene Brown

There were times when the difficulty of ongoing caregiving created a negative charge with my own sense of inadequacy. The task can be so daunting and so demanding that any of us who struggle with our sense of worth will feel eroded from time to time. We can do so little to stop the progression of age or illness, whether it's physical or emotional. And even though we intellectually know this, the feeling of helplessness is hard to accept and can sometimes feel like failure.

Self-care around this is so important. In order to be compassionate with our loved one, we must also be compassionate with ourselves. I often journaled about my own sense of not doing enough until I felt some clarity. I also often needed reassurance from my support team that I was indeed doing enough—in fact, doing a lot.

*Today I will take some time to re-center my sense of who I am. The more centered I am spiritually, the more my compassion will ring true for my loved one and still honor and know its limitations.*

## *January 20*

***"Setting boundaries is a way of taking care of myself. It doesn't make me mean, selfish, or uncaring..."***

—Christine Morgan

As caregivers, we are often signing up for a job—a labor of love—that is, by definition, lopsided. It is often hard to give ourselves permission to set limits or boundaries. Yet, if we don't set limits and protect our own needs, we will eventually become a not-very-good caregiver. Burnout, bitterness, and resentment are hallmarks of caregivers who haven't learned to set limits on how much of their own time and energy they can give.

It is necessary to find ways to take care of ourselves, even in the midst of intense needs on the part of another. An afternoon off, a day or two away, or a change of pace in any way can restore us to sanity. It is vital to find ways to let others help out when we need a break. It truly is not selfish; rather, it is self-care that keeps us going for the long haul.

*If I am feeling resentment, I can find a way to take care of myself and that tired part of me so that I can reconnect with my source of love for myself and my loved one.*

## *January 21*

***"Some days we need to dig beyond a sense of duty or external expectation to the deeper inpulse in our hearts that calls us to caregiving."***

—Patricial Hoolihan, *journal*

Impulse of heart. Before you is an important person in your life. No matter what mistakes he or she made along the way, no matter if at times the edges of your relationship feel frayed, before you stands a person to whom you feel connected. Your deepest impulse is to be there and to help in the ways that you can.

It is good to return to that impulse over and over again. It is the source of your energy and sustenance. It is what moves you to show up and to keep showing up. If your actions are motivated by the need to earn love or by the need to promote a certain self-image, your energy will often run thin. Your heart is the center of love, and from it emanates the energy of kindness.

*I will light a candle, pause, and remember to honor the impulse to love that has moved me to care for my loved one.*

## January 22

***" . . . [M]ature care emphasizes interactive, relational selves, it requires ongoing reflection. Such reflection concerns not only how to understand and respond to the other, but also to oneself, and can be described as a continuing self-reflection."***

—Tove Pettersen

There are academic studies about the nature and ethics of care—that's how important it is to humanity. Mature care is described as the kind of care that finds a balance between giving to another and taking care of oneself, of honoring the multiple relationships that are a part of this loved one's care.

Time to reflect is often hard to come by when one is caregiving a loved one and also juggling other commitments. Yet, it is important to pay attention to one's feelings and thoughts: that tug at the heart, that plunge into an old sense of inadequacy, that recurring struggle with guilt. Take a few moments when they arise to pay attention, to reflect. Do you need to reach out to your friend who understands your struggles with guilt and can help you let go of those feelings for today? Is the difficulty of your life today plunging you into a sense of inadequacy that is more of an old pattern than an accurate assessment? We all need to be supported, and ongoing reflection can help us reach out for what we need today. It is so important to understand and respond to ourselves, as well as to our loved one.

*I will take a few moments to honor and understand what I am feeling today and to care for those feelings in a concrete way.*

## *January 23*

***"Our greatest healer is sitting right under our nose, moving in and out—our breath."***

—Jacquelyn Small

One of the most simple and effective techniques for quieting anxiety is slowing down one's breath, taking in deep inhalations, counting to ten while paying attention to the breath. Anxiety is often a part of this path. Both of my parents dealt with anxiety, and I often felt anxious about their anxiety (it's contagious). Of course, there are medications to help with this as well. But when one's body and/or mind is deteriorating and previous abilities are slipping away, it is so understandable to feel anxiety. There are so many small losses, so much that is unknown about what lies ahead.

When so much is out of one's control, the focus on breath is a reminder. A reminder that the simple act of breathing is life-affirming, an ability to be appreciated. Take the time to slow your own breathing, to encourage your loved one to do the same. Even breathe together, a few deep inhalations and exhalations. Do it over again—until you calm your racing hearts. It is healing to return to the present moment in this way. It is healing to remember to appreciate the simple gift of breathing.

*Entering deeply and with gratitude into each present breath, by myself and with my loved one, is a wonderful antidote to anxiety about the unpredictable future.*

## *January 24*

**"When the music changes, so does the dance."**

—African proverb

My father loved music. In his prime, I would play piano, and he would sing song after song around the piano. As he grew older, he would sing one or two and then be too tired to carry on. But he always loved music. In his last weeks, through the care of hospice, a music therapist would come visit him. She knew all the oldie songs of his generation. He would sing slowly with her sometimes, and other times just listen to her and keep the beat with his fingers.

"Red sails in the sunset . . . " was one of his favorite lines. It evoked in me a beautiful image of this time in his life. Watching him sing, even haltingly, moved me to tears—in part because of our long history of sharing music, but also because I could feel the music touching him, connecting to years of memories, memories he was in some stage of leaving behind. I also heard the words and music more intimately than I ever had before. Those moments led me deep inside both the melody and the beautiful metaphor of the words. The long goodbyes are hard on our hearts but create many heart-opening moments. There are many ways and resources to bring music into our world.

*A moment of music that touches my loved one, in any form, can touch my own awareness of the rich emotion of this time we are sharing.*

# January 25

***"I didn't grow up saying 'I would like to be a caregiver.' But I have found caregiving to be the most important, profound job I've ever had."***

—Caroline Johnson

Most of us wonder at times or even on a daily basis about what matters in life, how to carve out meaning in the midst of our ordinary lives. We seek meaning in many ways over the course of our lives. The path of caregiving is not a glamorous one, and most often is not dreamed about or sought after. The need presents itself, and for a whole host of reasons, we respond to it.

This path, which is multifaceted with its many demands, also carries moments of profound meaning, as well as a continual, ongoing, almost invisible, sustained sense of meaning. If it is your parents you are caring for, then you are giving back what was given to you when you were a helpless child. If it is a spouse or friend or other relative, then you are giving back to an even wider circle of love and care. Distilled to its essence, life is a deep well of love that we draw from to help each other through the hard times. In that way, this arduous, less-than-glamorous, and ever-demanding choice to be a caregiver also rewards us daily with a deep and profound realization that our presence and caring matter and make a difference in both tangible and invisible ways.

*Today I will honor the profound moments this path gives me, the way it attunes me to how we human beings matter to one another. There is deep meaning in these moments that I will treasure for the rest of my life.*

## *January 26*

***"Like it or not, the tasks of elder care are largely divided along traditional gender lines. . . . It is what it is."***

—Jane Gross

If you are female and reading this, then you have probably already caught on to this reality. Maybe you look around you at a care facility or look at who steps forward in your family, and you are seeing mostly female. If you are a male reading this, then you are the exception, and most likely there are particular challenges for you because of this. We certainly hope there are more and more of you in the years to come. If you identify as neither or both, you too have probably noticed the high numbers of females visiting people in care facilities, no matter where you live.

Although much is happening in the world of gender roles and gender identities, some things are deeply entrenched. It's a good awareness to have. Change in this regard is worth promoting in any way we can. But it seemed to me, when I was an active caregiver, that fighting this was way beyond what I had in terms of energy or time. "It is what it is" became a way for me to just accept and to continue to embrace why I took on this role and why it was important to me. Perhaps at another time in our lives we can be change agents; for now, we are caregivers.

*Acceptance of systems that are mostly beyond my control will clear the way for me to remember why I am a caregiver to this special loved one in my life. This clarity infuses rather than detracts from my energy.*

## *January 27*

***"It is of course important to encourage the positive, but it is also crucial sometimes to allow ourselves to mourn."***

—Karen Armstrong

As meaningful as the caregiving journey can be and is, it is also lined and laced with sadness. Your loved one's loss is your own loss. So often we get caught up in the ideal of being always positive, but it is important to honor what is also authentic: the sadness of this journey. We don't need to impose an awareness of that on our loved one, but if they are in a space where they are feeling mournful, it's important to honor that. It's an authentic part of being human and a tangible aspect of this journey for both of you. When the sadness emerges, it is often asking to be tended to. Tending means honoring it for what it is and accepting its presence in a kind and understanding way.

Allowing oneself the space for mourning means allowing the tears to come, recognizing what they are about, and probably talking about those tears with someone who understands. It also means allowing our loved ones their moments of sadness too.

*Although a positive attitude is best most of the time, allowing the grief to come through and be expressed where and when it needs to is an integral, healing, and healthy part of this journey.*

## *January 28*

***"When we connect with compassionate motivation, we connect with our greatest inner resource: our basic goodness."***

—Kirsten DeLeo

Most of us who are caregivers would never call ourselves do-gooders; that is usually not a helpful way to see ourselves. But it is helpful to name and refresh the roots of our motivation from time to time. What drives us to step in where we see a need? What opens us to see the need? In the above writer's terms, it is our basic goodness. The term is both tangible and ecumenical.

There are other ways to say this: because we care, because we are caring people. Love is about giving and receiving. Our basic goodness describes the impulse to be a force for good in this world, to be a loving and caring presence. On some days, this sounds much easier than it actually is in the day-to-day living. But even on the hard days, we can remember that our goodness is a resource, an energy reserve. If we keep feeding it, it will keep feeding us with the energy we need for this journey.

*I will take time today to connect with my deeper motivations about giving care to my loved one; in this way, I remember and tap into this resource of goodness within me.*

## *January 29*

***"I am a traveler on a sacred journey through this one shining day."***

—Richard Wagamese

The word long sometimes comes to mind around the effort of caregiving. In many cases, weeks stretch into months and then into years. Some days are so packed with so many needs that the day itself feels long. These beautiful words from a thoughtful native writer remind us of the sacredness of this journey—through one shining day at a time.

Just for today, we can look around and find what is shining into and around us. Each day shimmers with some form of kindness or light, if we can open our eyes and hearts to it. There is the light shining in the eyes of the person we are caring for; no matter the ravages of time or sickness, it is a familiar light. And there is a beauty in that. Some people go far afield to hike on unknown trails; in caregiving, we are adventuring through the sacredness of small steps. What shines through it all is love.

*Today I will honor the sacredness of my chosen journey and open my heart to this shining day.*

## *January 30*

***"For everything there is a season, and a time for every matter under heaven."***

—Ecclesiastes 3:1

Time and timing are key components on this journey we share as caregivers with our loved ones. This well-known Biblical saying about there being a time and a season for everything can be a source of comfort. Often, along this path we need to just accept where our loved one is at—beyond providing comfort and attending to medical needs, much that is happening is beyond our control.

Timing is a factor we can turn over to the universal rhythm of a larger sense of the passages of time and seasons. This is a new season in our loved one's life, and in some way, the timing is just as it needs to be. Likewise, our own sense of what we need to do and when can be aided by an understanding of larger rhythms around us.

*I can trust that there is a season for everything and the season of our lives right now is blessed by its own perfect, if not always understood, timing.*

## *January 31*

***"Lord, make me an instrument of your peace; where there is hatred, let me sow love, . . . where there is despair, hope."***

—Prayer of St. Francis of Assisi

This simple and well-known prayer has a lot to say that pertains to us caregivers. To be an instrument of peace means that we are encouraged to come to this role with a sense of inner peace. Clarity is key. Most of us need to ponder to some extent why we are drawn to this role and why our skills or availability match the need that we see. Perhaps we even need to be clear about the existence of this need, as others might see it differently. It's important to access the part of us that is drawn to this role, ultimately, out of love. In order to sow love, we need to be aware of its source within us.

Love intertwines with hope. We will experience days when our loved one or our own worn-down selves are feeling hopeless, sometimes even desperate. Like the well that draws from somewhere deep below the earth's surface, love can help us reach down through the layers of life to find hope in every moment—especially the moments where we are expressing care and love for another.

*As I approach this day, as a caregiver, let me remember to be an instrument of peace, love, and hope.*

# February

## *February 1*

***"Sometimes there's nothing to do but surrender."***

—Tosha Silver

Many of us push ourselves to a hard edge before we become willing to surrender. We are people who want to exert our will, fight for what we believe in. There are many times in life when that is the most effective path. But there are also times in life when one must learn to let go of what we cannot change. Truly letting go, surrendering, is both more difficult and more simple than it sounds.

Some days, as a caregiver I needed to surrender to the powerful feelings I was having, not all of them very noble. Some days, I needed to surrender what I wished would happen for my mother and needed to stop imposing my will upon her day. Although I often resisted surrender, when I gave in to it, there was a huge relief. Acceptance flowed in, a much more peaceful state of being than fighting for a specific outcome.

*If I am feeling at my wits' end, surrender is calling to me. I can reach for its sweet relief and trust that beyond surrender lies the grace born of acceptance.*

## *February 2*

***"Caregiving is a deeply ingrained human response to suffering."***

—Henri Nouwen

One of the inspiring aspects of COVID-19 has been the spotlight on how human beings care for one another in times of duress. In our cities, in various states, and across the globe there have been synchronized and touching tributes of appreciation to all the healthcare workers who have been the heroes in the midst of the pandemic. In spite of social distancing, humans found ways to appreciate those who work to alleviate suffering. Many other kinds of workers have also shown their loyalty to providing for the needs of their fellow humans in so many ways.

Despite all the difficulties and all the friction of differing points of view, there has rightfully been much attention paid to how we care for one another, especially the sick, the vulnerable, and the dying. Caregiving falls along the same path, although it is often given less attention or applause. We who choose this path are responding, in a deep and deeply human way, to the suffering of a loved one.

*When doubts creep in, I can rely on the knowledge and understanding that my role as a caregiver is rooted in a personal and yet universal response to a loved one's suffering.*

## *February 3*

***"Breath is the bridge which connects life to consciousness, which unites your body to your thoughts."***

—Thich Nhat Hanh

There are days as a caregiver when breath lodges in the upper reaches of one's chest and your body begins to feel separate from your anxious mind. Fast shallow breathing is a sure sign of this. There are a variety of breathing techniques that help lower stress and anxiety; the simplest and most accessible one, no matter where you are, is to inhale deeply through your nose in a way that fills your diaphragm and then slowly exhale through pursed lips. If you do this 5 to 10 times, slowly, you will note a physiological response in your body. This is a simple and effective way to move your body out of the shallow breathing that accompanies stress and anxiety.

This is a tool that is accessible to all, and it is a way to bring your body, mind, and heart together. As you breathe, you create the opening to connect with the deep truths you are experiencing as a caregiver. What has been frozen in your body thaws and begins to flow. In this way, each one of us can move ourselves into a deeper awareness of our humanity and the gift of life—through breath. It is always possible to get there.

*When I feel uptight, I can relax my shoulders, draw a deep breath in through my nose, and slowly exhale through my mouth. In this way, I let in the light and let go of the darkness, over and over again.*

## *February 4*

***"Learning to be compassionate toward ourselves is a lifelong process. We learn and forget, learn and forget."***

—Gail Straub

My hardest days as a caregiver were the days I felt guilty about drawing a boundary or the days I felt woefully inadequate to the needs at hand. We all have different variations of the demons that tell us in any number of ways that we are not good enough. Like birds hiding in the bushes, they will be flushed into sight and flight by the demands of caregiving.

It helps to name these voices that tear at us, and to get a reality check from somewhere outside of our own heads: a good friend, our spiritual source, a fellow caregiver. In this way, the negative voices have less power over us and have less power to drain our vital energy. Over and over again, as caregivers, we are given opportunities to be compassionate toward what is ragged within us; each time we remember that, we heal ourselves toward wholeness.

*I am grateful for the way caregiving keeps reminding me, over and over again, how important it is to practice kindness toward myself.*

## *February 5*

***"The most important conversations***
***we'll have are with our fingers . . .***
***Your fingers will grip mine***
***To say things words can't describe."***

—rupi kaur

When I was caring for my mom, I was healthy except for occasional short sicknesses. But at one time much earlier in my life, I had been gravely ill. My parents, aunts, and uncle gathered around my hospital bed before I went in for surgery. Someone held my hands, and they all held hands around the circle. Their voices joined in prayer were enormously comforting to my scared soul.

In later years, I tended to each one of them. In some ways I was still thanking them for being there at my time of facing a huge darkness; their presence and love helped pull me back among the living. Their hands holding mine said it all. When it was my turn to hold their hands, the love going back and forth pulsed in the current moments but also in the depth of connection from the past.

*Holding hands, letting fingers convey love and loyalty, is a gift that swiftly crosses an ocean of time.*

## February 6

***" . . . [S]urvey all my friends from the acute trauma ward, and they will tell you that they live to give a halting hug, or to speak a word of grace to another."***

—Rabbi Yehudah Fine

The beauty of being close to someone who is aging or—due to illness of any sort—whose skills are diminishing is that their lives are being distilled into what is most essential. It is always a good reminder to be around this. So many of us get carried away with other distractions, with sometimes meaningless worries. At life's essence, what really matter the most to any of us humans are compassionate gestures or kind words.

In the world of caregiving, this becomes clear. The desire for prestige or material possession fades; presence matters. This can be in person or via telephone—or in this day and age, FaceTime. Presence, taking the time to connect, matters. Every time I hugged my mother's thin bones and she leaned in to my strength, I felt the power of that hug.

*Today let me remember how we all live for a kind hug or compassionate word from another. Let my caregiving role and the presence of my loved one be the reminder.*

## February 7

***"Drum sounds rise on the air,***
***and with them, my heart.***
***A voice inside the beat says,***
***I know you are tired,***
***But come.***
***This is the way."***

—Rumi

It is called digging deep. It is knowing your inner flame burns brighter than it sometimes feels. It is the challenge of the days when your motor feels run down, but there are just a few more things that you must tend to before even thinking of taking a break. Yes. Those days happen. Those situations arise.

Drum sounds rising on the air are the whispers of a wisdom beyond our tired brains. And a voice inside the drumbeat could be the whisper of an ancestor or our own source of wisdom. This is the way. Forward. One loving step at a time. Some days and moments of caregiving are truly akin to the last miles of a long-distance run. One foot in front of the other. Let the goal lift the weight of tiredness enough to keep moving forward on your way.

*In the air around me, there is a quiet drumbeat; from its rhythm, I will find the energy to do what I need to do today.*

## *February 8*

***"When to shift from pushing against limits to making the best of them is not often readily apparent. . . . Helping my father through the struggle to define that moment was simultaneously among the most painful and most privileged experiences of my life."***

—Atul Gawande

Gawande, a doctor well-versed in working with an aging population, brought both his medical experience and an open heart to caring for his father. For everyone who is aging or dealing with a disease that is weakening them, there comes a time when pushing oneself to fight limits doesn't work anymore. Perhaps there are many such moments. It is as if a lifetime of training to push and excel suddenly needs to be completely re-wired toward acceptance of what is and cannot be changed.

As caregivers, we watch and help our loved ones as they move through this enormous transition. As Gawande so clearly says, it is painful to watch a loved one grapple with losses. And yet, if we can encourage them toward acceptance, relief in the form of a new and quieter kind of courage has the potential to replace resistance. The river of acceptance is a peaceful one, though it may take traversing wild waters to get there.

*No matter where my loved one is in this process, I am grateful for the privilege of all that I am learning as I share this time with him or her.*

## *February 9*

**"Music is the moonlight in the gloomy night of life."**

—Jean Paul Friedrich Richter

I have a friend who is really good at putting together collections of recorded music according to mood or theme. When his sister was pregnant, he created a labor tape, which was enormously comforting to her through a long and difficult labor. When his father was diagnosed with cancer and had to do regular long hours of chemo, he put together several hours of soothing music for him. The music helped transform the long hours of watching the medicine drip into his body into something that felt quietly radiant—like moonlight.

Whether we are caregiving a loved one who has cancer, has had a stroke, or has other health or memory issues, music is a common denominator for healing and uplifting one's spirit. There is research around what kinds of music are soothing or energizing, but most musical taste is personal. You probably know what kind of music soothes your loved ones, so find that friend who can put a playlist together and help your loved one get set up electronically to listen to music when they are alone. Whether it's jazz or classical piano or sing-alongs from musicals or beloved hymns, music will lighten anyone's day.

*I can find a way to make music available for my loved one. In gloomy moments, the music becomes a tool that enters their heart with a beautiful light—the sheen of moonlight.*

## *February 10*

***"May I befriend the unwanted parts of myself***
***And continually learn wisdom from them."***

—Joyce Rupp

For those of us for whom the caregiving path is a long one, it often invites to the surface some parts of ourselves we would rather not see. To name a few of my own such parts: resentment, a sense of inadequacy for the huge task at hand, frustration. These may arise due to a particular circumstance or just due to the fragility that is born of fatigue.

The rugged and beautiful challenge is to befriend those difficult traits in ourselves. Befriending is the opposite of judging. Befriending takes into consideration the deeper truths beneath these feelings. Befriending begins with acceptance. The more kindness we can extend to ourselves, the deeper our ability to feel and share compassion. In these ways, we are continually learning more about our own human depth of emotion; we are continually asked to open our hearts.

*There is much potential wisdom to be absorbed as I notice, accept, and befriend my own frustrations on this challenging path.*

## *February 11*

**"Mature care prevents self-sacrifice from becoming habitual."**

—Tove Pettersen

For most of us drawn into the world of caregiving, we struggle with knowing where the line is when we are giving too much of ourselves away. Of course, caregiving is demanding. And the line is a slippery one, changing from day to day. Often, we give too much away before we see that line we probably should not have crossed. A burned out, exhausted, sick caregiver is not of much good use to anyone.

The idea of mature care incorporates an awareness of the ongoing need for self-care. Mature care is thoughtful in that we learn to give more intentionally rather than habitually. Yes, as caregivers, we often sacrifice time for ourselves, but we can also make time for it. Grab it when we can. One friend of mine says even ten minutes to herself in the morning helps center her for the tasks of the day.

*Rejuvenation comes when I find ways to create self-care, in the midst of a demanding, somewhat self-sacrificing journey.*

*February 12*

***"'Happy New Year!' (Chinese: 新年好呀; pinyin: Xīn Nián Hǎo Ya; ) is a popular children's song for the New Year holiday. The melody is similar to the American folk song, "Oh My Darling, Clementine": "Happy New Year! Happy New Year! Happy New Year to you all! We are singing; we are dancing. Happy New Year to you all!"***

—Google

The first day of Chinese New Year begins on the new moon that appears between January 21 and February 20. In 2020, the first day of the Chinese New Year was on Saturday, January 25, but in 2021 it will be celebrated on February 12. One of the most important shared meals of the year celebrates this day. Beautiful paper lanterns are lit; gifts are given. People clean their homes to sweep away ill-fortune and to make way for incoming luck and blessings.

Wherever any of us are during the new moon at the end of January and early February, we can celebrate the idea of a new year, of welcoming good luck into our future. The shared meal is a reminder that how so many of us celebrate life and love is by sharing a meal. Traditional meals hold special meaning. This is true for song as well: the melody for "Oh My Darling, Clementine" is easy to sing, melodic, and full of innocence. Pair it with the words, and we are singing and dancing and one's heart is lifted.

*Today I will let the awareness of Chinese New Year fill my day with a special sense of the possibility of good things to come.*

## *February 13*

***"None of us, including me, ever do great things. But we can all do small things, with great love, and together we can do something wonderful."***

—Mother Teresa

There are myths that surround the role of caregiving. One of them is that caregivers are saintly people. Such a standard for this role is not very helpful. Even Mother Teresa, who has been canonized as a saint for all of her charitable works and ways of living, didn't see herself in this light. She didn't see herself as doing great things, although of course most of the world sees her differently.

Her attitude and sense of self is so telling. She promotes teamwork. She advances the idea that small things done with great love can really make a difference. Small things done with great love. I think back on the many visits to the eye doctor or regular doctor that my sister and I did with our Mom. I think back on the many special gifts she received from all of my siblings, the way she cherished visits from all. All of those small things done in a spirit of love helped carry her to the end on waves of comfort, and even joy, surfacing between the hardships.

*Together, with great love, I and the others who are helping me on this caregiving journey can really make a wonderful difference.*

## *February 14*

***"Let us carve gems out of our strong hearts and let them light our path to love."***

—Rumi

The journey of the caregiver is definitely a journey of the heart. We are accompanying a loved one through a very difficult time; both of us will deal with vulnerabilities all along the way. This is the alchemy of love, burning through the pain and disappointment and forging something stronger in the end.

My favorite aunt once said to me, "You are a gem of a human being." I hold onto that. And I often remembered it as I cared for that aunt and for the other elders in my family. Each was a gem, unique and lovable in his or her own way. The way we connected was heart to heart. The loving heart is truly a jewel, and caregiving—like a tumbler for raw gems—polishes that jewel to reveal our true radiance.

*Caring for my loved one is providing me with a daily way to polish and tumble into luminescence the jewel of my heart.*

## *February 15*

***"All conditioned things are subject to decay. Strive for your liberation with diligence."***

—Buddha

Around this time of year, Buddhists across the world celebrate Nirvana Day. It is a day to honor the death of their prophet, Buddha. Buddhism revolves around seeking inner peace and peace in the world by accepting the reality that life is always changing. Practitioners work on finding and maintaining a balance that is positive and hopeful, of working to let go of all the ways our minds and the ways of the world fight against such peace.

I find that one of the most helpful premises of Buddhism is working on accepting the inevitability of change. As caregivers, we are adapting on an almost daily basis to changes; rather than fighting this or wishing it were otherwise, the tradition of Buddhism reminds us to work on acceptance. A worthy goal is to liberate ourselves from being thrown off-balance by the changes that come our way.

*I can learn from the philosophy of Buddhism, even if I am not very familiar with it, to accept the changes that come my way and to keep seeking a peaceful heart in the face of those changes.*

## *February 16*

***"Feelings of guilt are unavoidable when we care for a loved one. The best we can do is focus on the many good efforts we make, forgive ourselves for our mistakes, and continue doing our best."***

—Barry Jacobs and Julia Mayer

I can say for certain that one of the hardest feelings I dealt with during my many months of caring for my mother was guilt. Like the stereotype goes, she was good at inviting it. But the responsibility was mine on whether to take it on or not. Still, most of us struggle with guilt when it comes to caregiving. We run into limits of time and emotional patience. Sometimes we need to say no for reasons that are completely understandable but are not necessarily understood by our loved one. I remember once or twice closing the door to my mother's apartment in her assisted living place, resting my head against the wall, and telling myself, "It's okay. You did the best you can for today. That is enough. In fact, it is more than enough."

When we are in it for the long haul, we need to find ways to take care of ourselves without plunging into guilt when we disappoint our loved one. When guilt does rear its head, we can learn ways to let it go, to observe it but not let it get us down. In doing so, we are ultimately protecting our ability to continue to care for our loved one.

*The guiltometer may kick in, but I can learn how to quiet it more quickly by remembering that the limits I set help keep me sane and healthy enough to come back the next time in good spirits.*

## *February 17*

***"As we journey out of ashes to Easter joy, dispel the darkness of our hearts and shine your light within us so that we may proclaim unending praise to you."***

—Teri Larson, *Evening Thanksgiving Prayer*

The Lenten season begins with Ash Wednesday, with the invocation "Remember that you are dust and to dust you shall return." The blessing of the ashes reminds us of our humble and universal births and deaths—what we humans all have in common. The annual journey from darkness to light is one that is reflected both seasonally and also daily. In this beautiful prayer, we are asking for help to dispel the darkness, to reflect light in our souls.

Whatever name we use for a source of spirit and love can be used here. Unending praise to God, to a Higher Power, to the Great Mystery, to Mother Earth, to Love. Here is a reminder to ask for such help. In the dark days of caregiving, we can continually seek and ask for spiritual help in dispelling the darkness, in being able to see where the light is shining, in being able to love in steadfast and deep ways.

*I can praise the power of love today in my role as a caregiver by seeking spiritual help to do so.*

## *February 18*

**"In a perfect world, before a crisis, I would have found—and urge you to find—an internist, or better still, a geriatrician or a geriatric care manager."**

—Jane Gross

There is a lot to be said for having good professionals who can help you with the care of your loved one. Sometimes such a person or persons is found ahead of time, but more often it is a crisis that really makes the search for professional help happen. Inevitably, this is part of caregiving—finding the resources and the professionals that your loved one needs. This requires the action of reaching out, asking for suggestions, talking to people, and doing some research.

There are resources available no matter where you live. It is true that a city often provides more resources and more specialized resources. This can be a challenge if you live in a more rural environment. However, often the smaller towns can provide a more personal professionalism. If you can see your loved one needs more help than he or she is receiving, it is so important to do what you can to change that and/or to enlist help in doing so. Finances are a factor here, but often solutions come in surprising ways.

*I can be creative and proactive about seeing that my loved one is well taken care of medically. Reaching out with questions and asking for help is always a good place to begin.*

## *February 19*

***"It was the spring of hope, it was the winter of despair."***

—Charles Dickens

I have a vivid memory of going through a difficult time with our father. During a crisis, he was hospitalized, and we all—my siblings, our mother, and myself—thought we could breathe a sigh of relief for a few nights. Instead, he was released the next day. Hospitals have their rules, and at that time it seemed against every grain of common sense that we could see. Still, getting him settled back home was a relief for him. The crisis impelled the next decision-making efforts, which turned out to be made just in the nick of time, before his health further deteriorated.

There were times when crisis followed comfort so quickly, starting the cycle all over again, that we could barely catch our breaths. Hope and despair seemed to be twin ends of a shared teeter-totter. The more we found our way to a centered balance point, the more we could find calm.

*Inside the winter of despair, we can always reach for and find the hope of spring.*

## *February 20*

***"Although it was my job to speak for them (my parents) when they couldn't speak for themselves, the most important (and often most challenging) thing was to remember they were going through a much more difficult rite of passage than I was."***

—Caroline Johnson

It's an odd position to be in, to be the one advocating for and sometimes speaking for our loved ones who, for any number of reasons, are not able to protect their own interests or speak strongly enough for their own needs. They need us to speak up in order to be heard out in the world. But this does not in any way diminish who they are. It is key to listen to our loved ones—they can speak to us, even if they don't have the strength to speak to the larger world.

As unnerving as this might be for we who are caregiving, it is essential to remember the rite of passage our loved ones are moving through. When one pauses, we can feel how profound such a change is, first for our loved one and then for us as well. Being aware of that shift, whether it's sudden or more likely gradual, helps us to step in with empathy and compassion.

*The rite of passage my loved one is going through deserves my respect, even as—and especially as—I grapple with filling in where my voice is needed. I am speaking for him or her, not over and above them.*

## *February 21*

***"Allow nature's peace to flow into you as sunshine flows into trees."***

—John Muir

On edge might be a good way to describe how I often felt when I was most deeply immersed as a caregiver. Balancing schedules, my needs, my children's needs, my work, and my mother's care was truly a juggling act. Some of the moments of calm that live on in my memory are connected to nature. Taking my mom for a short walk with her walker when the autumn sun shone upon us; both of us absorbing and longing for its kindness. Bundling her up and pushing her out for fresh air on a cold day when she was wheelchair bound. The way she took deep breaths, grateful for the fresh air, which allowed me to also deeply feel that simple gratitude.

The night my father died, I stepped outside to a sky full of stars. The earlier snowfall was followed by wind, which blew all the clouds away. Every twinkling star felt like a friend to me in that luminous, and in some ways lonesome, moment.

*Nature's peace and beauty are always there for us; when we caregivers feel longing or need, we can reach for this bounty in all its many forms and allow its peace to enter our tired bones.*

## *February 22*

**"Limitless undying love which shines around me like a million suns, it calls me on and on across the universe."**

—John Lennon

What calls us forward on this journey as a caregiver? Of course, it's love. In this beautiful image and melody by Lennon, we are reminded of the abundance of love shining all around us—limitless, undying. I remember when my children were babies and sometimes they called out in the night or were sick and needed lots of care. I was tired, but there was never any question about finding the energy to be there and do what needed to be done. Even then, I imagined this deep well of love I could dig into and draw from when I needed to.

That well is there, and on days when we need to dig deep to find the energy for the day's demands, we can remember that love is a deep well. When we truly need it, we will find it to be limitless and undying. We can hear it calling us on and on across the sunlit route of our day. Its energy is as dependable as the sun.

*As a caregiver and as a human being, I have a deep well of love to draw from; when the needs are high and the energy is low, I can pull from this deep and abiding resource.*

## *February 23*

***"My caregiver mantra was:***
***1. Stay positive.***
***2. Speak from compassion and with love.***
***3. Hold the truth.***
***4. Ask for and be open to grace and mercy."***

—Kris Berggren

Sometimes as caregivers we are seen as the "bad guy"—the one who delivers hard news or helps implement change that our loved one is resistant or reluctant toward. This is a particularly challenging situation. It's a difficult job even when one is appreciated, so to be at the receiving end of resistance or distrust requires extra emotional strength and stamina.

The above four points were created to help this particular caregiver through such a situation. Staying positive was a goal, to not be deflected by negative energy coming at her. Holding the truth was and is always important, but to speak the truth in tones of compassion and love is the only way to (eventually) be heard—and is perhaps how we most want to hear ourselves. Lastly, this is a journey where grace and mercy often arrive in surprising ways, especially the more one attunes to, looks for, and takes in the possibility.

*Today I will remain positive, speak the truth with compassion, and be open to merciful moments and gifts of grace.*

## *February 24*

***"A person with cancer dies in increments, and a part of you slowly dies with them."***

—Terry Tempest Williams

Love opens us to warmth, light, joy, and heartbreak. Love deepens our days in innumerable ways. Yet, love and loss are intertwined. The gorgeous weaving of threads of camaraderie and shared experiences is also partly threaded with concern and losses connected to our loved ones. This is why for so many parents, bittersweet tears fall when their children leave home to find their way in the world. Such a moment overflows with waves of love and loss.

When we accompany a loved one through a health crisis—cancer and other forms—we are a part of this slowly dying process. Nothing about that is easy. Yet, the alternative, to leave one to suffer alone, is unthinkable for most of us. Love calls us to be a companion. Love calls us to compassion. Love is the boat within which floats the shared sadness as well as the richness of all the beautiful times shared.

*I will take some time today to honor the sadness that is part of this journey. My feelings of loss are an integral part of the beautiful tapestry called love.*

## *February 25*

***"All they need is someone who stays present no matter what, who is real and, most importantly, is kind."***

—Kirsten DeLeo

The "they" refers to those who are nearing the end, whether it be weeks or months away. Being present to that sobering reality, even if it isn't talked about, requires some strength and courage. It means being real and being kind in the face of honest conversations or another's physical pain. It means simply sitting and being with hard questions or difficult-to-express emotions.

Many days, our presence is all that matters—not answers that we can provide, not fake bravado. What our loved ones are facing is the great mystery, and everyone enters it alone. Imagine approaching a lonely, dark hole, and then imagine the comfort of someone holding your hand as you face it or sitting beside you as you wait for it. Imagine how comforting a hug would be, or a smile, or just a quiet presence beside you.

*Today the only kindness that matters is that in my time with my loved one, I am open-hearted and able to be fully there, listening, even to what is unspoken.*

## *February 26*

**"Want to be happy? Stop trying to be perfect."**

—Brene Brown

Perfectionism worms its way into many parts of our lives. It is almost a sure bet that our personal struggles with perfectionism will rise to the surface in our time as caregivers. It almost always is accompanied by a voice that tells us either we aren't doing enough or we are not doing it well enough. Our time as a caregiver gives us a chance to wrestle with and hopefully face down our perfectionistic tendencies.

It is possible to rebut the perfectionist ideal, to clearly and firmly tell ourselves that we are doing the best we can and to tell ourselves that what we are doing is truly enough. In this way, it becomes possible to feel a glimmer of happiness. In this way, we can acknowledge what we are accomplishing, most likely under difficult circumstances. Happiness and contentment are possible every day, especially when I can let go of the false ideal of perfectionism.

*Rather than questioning what more I could be doing, I will cherish and honor the care I already give from my humble, loving, and imperfect self.*

## *February 27*

***"You yourself, as much as anyone in the entire Universe, deserve your own love and affection."***

—Buddha

One of my friends read Julie Andrews' biography, and as Julie was making her way through the world, she often told herself, "Good job, Julie." We all loved this, and so when one or the other of us is doing something well, we will say, "Good job, Julie." Not one of us is named Julie, but this only amuses us. This is just to say, we borrowed that idea of appreciating our own efforts and each other's.

For me, it was a reminder to appreciate and cheer on my own best efforts at life—even, and especially, the small steps. It's a concrete way to love myself, to show affection for myself. One way to honor the caregiving journey is to acknowledge the good job we are doing. It takes a lot of effort, and it's important to appreciate this effort in ourselves.

*I will pause to reflect and remind myself I am doing a good job—the best job I can do— and it is making the world, my world, a better place to be.*

## *February 28*

***"There is no closer bond than the one that gratefulness celebrates, the bond between giver and thanksgiver. Everything is a gift. Grateful living is a celebration of the universal give-and-take of life, a limitless yes to belonging."***

—Brother David Stendal-Rast

There is a powerful sense of belonging that happens in a caregiving relationship. There's a sense of purpose and a deep sense of connection. In my experience, there was often a fluidity between giver and thanksgiver. A mutual flow of appreciation was possible for gifts exchanged in the moment and also back across the sweep of time. It always helped to remember those gifts across time.

Caregiving is a long moment in time inside of which we all celebrate the give and take that is so much a part of life. In a world where many feel lonely and isolated, the connection between loved one and caregivers is a powerful center, a hearth to gather around, a warmth that creates rippling waves of meaning.

*I am grateful for the give and take between myself and my loved one and for the deep universal sense of belonging it gives both of us.*

## *February 29*

***"This day is added to the calendar in leap years as a corrective measure, because the Earth does not orbit the sun in precisely 365 days."***

—Wikipedia

Any journey that demands as much of ourselves as caregiving needs corrective measures from time to time. Built into our human and scientific understanding of the earth's orbit is the corrective measure of leap day. Very few things in life are perfectly symmetrical or perfect in any way. In the configuration of how we plot time, how we assess the passage of a year, a corrective measure is built in. This is instructive in many ways.

It feels like an extra day—a day perhaps for reflection, for balancing out our own unevenness or imperfect rotations. Of course, we need to do so way more often than once every four years, but leap day reminds us to take some extra time. Perhaps our impatience needs correcting, perhaps we need to replace discouragement with a deeper sense of hope. Perhaps we need to reach out to someone we can trust to correct a feeling of being alone.

*Leap day—a reminder that I can reach for corrections when I feel out of balance or skewed in some way that prevents me from feeling whole.*

# March

## *March 1*

**"We are so afraid of the waters within us that we often tense as soon as we see tears, asking what's wrong, when perhaps we need to ask . . . what do you see?"**

—Mark Nepo

Tears are a part of this journey. At times they may be your tears, and other times, the tears of the person you are caring for. Yet, tears can make us nervous. They often invoke fear or discomfort. One day, I walked into my mom's room, and she was in tears. I probably did ask what was wrong—I don't remember exactly—but it did open up a tender moment between us. There was much for her to be sad about: she was a widow after a decades-long marriage, her living situation had changed, she had lost many friends, her physical abilities were more and more challenged, and ultimately she was also looking at her own mortality. That is a lot of loss.

Tears are an opening into this loss. Although our first instinct might be nervousness, it is also an opening into the truth and an opportunity for sharing and expressing deep emotions your loved one is feeling. Also, such a moment allows you to remember the potency of the journey the two of you are sharing. So often that gets lost in the many details of daily life.

*If my loved one overflows in tears, there is a chance to ask, "What is he or she seeing?" I hope for the strength to let go of fear and embrace the opening.*

## *March 2*

***"There is no way you should allow your parent to spend a night alone in an emergency room if you can possibly avoid it."***

—Jane Gross

My sister and I proudly say, with great relief now that it's over, that we were with our mother when she did have to spend those hours in an emergency room. They are some of my most vivid memories. No one ends up in an ER unless something difficult has happened: her list included broken bones, pneumonia, and influenza. ERs are very difficult places; often everyone is overworked, and they are understaffed. It's a place where advocacy is needed—for a hospital room to open up as soon as possible, for the necessary tests and drugs to be administered.

We were lucky enough to often have each other to help work our way through this experience. Everything about it was hard: watching our mother suffer, trying to figure out the next best step, standing around an antiseptic room, waiting. But it was clear that for our vulnerable, sick, or in pain mother to be there alone was not something either of us could abide. So we kept her company, we relieved each other to go to the restroom or the snack machine, and we helped figure out and execute the next move. I often felt overstretched, tired, and hungry. In the end, I am deeply grateful that I had a sister to go through the experience with and that we did not leave our shrinking, 90-something, sick mother alone to deal with the vagaries of a busy night in the ER.

*The ER is a scary place for any patient, and if I can possibly be there to soften the experience for my loved one, then that is a gift in the moment and one to be grateful for in the future.*

## *March 3*

***"What matters to them now are little things, the things we often don't notice because we are speeding along in the fast lane, planning what comes next."***

—Kirsten DeLeo

I found a surprising duality inside of the caregiving experience. On one hand, my life felt crazy busy. I was teaching, had a teenager to tend to, and was making an hour-long round-trip drive to my mother's assisted living facility as many as four times a week. It was not unusual to be awake at 5:00 a.m. to read my students' papers or to respond to the most current early morning emergency phone call from either my sister or my mother. My mind was a map of how to fit in all of what needed doing.

Whew. But oddly, when I spent time with my mother, when we got past basic needs that had to be addressed, we entered what I began to think of as slow time. A cup of tea was often the focus. In the time it took to boil water, get the mugs out, and scrounge for a small and simple treat, we both slowed down. The to-do list evaporated. Nothing else mattered except making the tea and sitting together as we let the warm liquid comfort us . . . as we let conversation flow or silence settle in. These moments seemed to make her most happy and content. The bright spot in her day was a moment of calm in mine—an oasis in the midst of busyness.

*Being with our loved ones is an opportunity to take a break from the speed of life, from the relentless to-do list. Savor the break—allow your loved one to remind you of the core of what is really important.*

## *March 4*

***"Love is the bridge."***

—Stephen Levine

There are many challenges along the caregiving road. Decisions require research and time; there are continual adjustments in the needs department, health crises arise, there is emotional fallout for both the receiver and giver of care. And, above all, it can be an endurance run. Time and again, the route through the challenge is to draw on our resources of love. Love is a well of energy that plummets deep inside the earth.

For me, it often evoked the time when I had babies. I remembered being so tired, but if my baby was in distress, there I was. No question about it. The energy welled up in response to the need. But beneath the energy was the pulsating depth of love.

*When need arises, I can trust that I am able to draw from a deep well of love: love for my loved one, love for my own sense of self, and love for this gift of shared life.*

## *March 5*

***"And though it (caregiving) is certainly not an easy task, caregiving changes you, makes you more human. We all need more of that."***

—Caroline Johnson

I have observed that many people who take on the role of caregiver are very competent. We tend to be capable, generous, and kind. That could be a gross exaggeration; however, I believe there is truth in it. Sometimes caregivers fall into a category of being saint-like, which of course is impossible to keep up. So what keeps us more human than saintly? It is grappling with the difficult parts of ourselves that surface when caregiving.

For me, it was often a sense of inadequacy. Since the needs were so huge and ever-changing, the experience tugged at a basic sense of mine that I was not enough, not doing enough, not doing it well enough. Some days, I felt resentful. In order to keep going and to regain a spirit that felt more loving, I needed to face this part of myself. Sometimes I did so in writing, sometimes in talking to a trusted friend or professional. The experience often dropped me into my core, where I met my humanity and grappled with finding ways to both gently accept and transform. To do so, I had to reach in and out: gentle guidance always helped.

*This journey as a caregiver deepens my sense of humanity. Rather than brush aside what comes up, I can find ways to accept, forgive, and heal myself a little bit each day.*

# *March 6*

***"We bring music to those who are on the edge—still in this world but on their way to the next one."***

—Threshold Singers

One of my discoveries along my journey as a caregiver was how many services there are available. I had no idea. Every need we bumped into, there was a service already created to fill that need. Not only was this true in the medical world, but also churches and other communities provide services. And not all of these services cost money.

I realized that my church choir had a smaller group who was available as "threshold singers." Since then, I have found out that many church choirs do this, and also groups who are not connected to a church. I contacted them, they sent me a list of potential songs and hymns, and I let them know which ones would be most meaningful to my mother. These amazing people and singers drove to her care facility. We had set it up for them to sing to her in the community room. All residents were invited. Can I possibly describe what it felt like to stand near my mom, my hand on her shoulder, as she gazed proudly at the singers her daughter had organized? Around the room were a few people in wheelchairs and others who found chairs and a place to store their walkers or cane. A few made it in on their own power. When the singers opened with "Amazing Grace," I saw tears in many an eye. Such an array of human beings, many of them so physically vulnerable. All were moved by the music, myself included.

*Let me be open to creative possibilities along this journey. There are many resources that will help brighten both my life and that of my loved one.*

## *March 7*

***"If you are weary, may you be aroused by passion and purpose."***

—Elizabeth Lesser

I think of my time as a caregiver as very meaningful. I deeply felt my purpose. There are days when I still, years later, palpably miss that sense of clear purpose. Yet, I would be the first to admit that there were also days when I wasn't sure if what I was doing was enough or enough of the right kind of action. Some days, my clarity was fogged over by exhaustion or feeling pulled in too many different directions.

It is helpful to find ways to remember our sense of purpose. What is the source of our desire to travel this road with our loved one? Whether it's love for him or her, to honor a long legacy of connection, or to fill a needed space in a family configuration, there is a source. And that source connects to a passion of love and caring. Remembering this source ourselves and being around people who can underscore and encourage its importance are essential to keeping that sense of meaning lit.

*The next time I light a candle, I will remember the source that nourishes me as I share this time and this journey with my loved one.*

## *March 8*

***"Even in the midst of total chaos, pain, and dysfunction, love is calling us to a higher experience and expression."***

—Iyanla Vanzant

No matter what our history is with our loved one, there most likely have been challenges along the way, tensions, differences of opinion. Everyone's personality can be edgy at times, and this can be exacerbated by pain, sickness, and aging. So it is only human to have days when you, the caregiver, feel impatient or irritated. It's very human.

It helps to know yourself in this way, to have someone in your life who you can complain to and let off the steam of irritation. But just as you wouldn't want your impatience to affect the gentleness with which you would hold a baby, so most caregivers want to find ways to prevent such normal human irritation from clouding over the genuine love you have for this person. It is possible to visualize putting the irritation in a small box until you can unpack it in a respectful way, clearing the path for loving action.

*Sometimes it takes conscious effort to clear away the irritation and to answer the higher call to love—ultimately, this feels better to me and to my loved one.*

## *March 9*

***"The willingness to show up changes us. It makes us a little braver each time."***

—Brene Brown

We caregivers have chosen this role, this journey, which requires that we show up and keep showing up. There is a richness to this practice of showing up. Sometimes I was nervous or hesitant before I walked in the door to my mother's assisted living facility. What challenges might greet me that day: how might she be feeling physically or emotionally, what problems might have arisen since our last visit, would I be able to lift her spirits if she were feeling down?

Crossing the threshold was my way of entering that role fully. And each time, I learned that I could handle the day's challenges. Some days this came easily. Some days I fought for it. Some days I needed to reach out for help, when I was with her or later in the day. I often did feel braver each time I crossed back over that threshold to the other parts of my life.

*Showing up is a huge part of the courage we inhabit as caregivers. We can give ourselves credit for all the small, daily steps that account for the ways we show up.*

## *March 10*

***" . . . 'it's absolutely tearing me apart that I can't reach out and hug my mother,' [Jillian] Van Hefty said. 'I don't want her to feel abandoned.'"***

—as quoted in *Star Tribune March* 29, 2020. Article by Chris Serres

During the stay-at-home orders of COVID-19, most caregivers were no longer allowed in to visit their loved ones. This goes against all of our caring instincts. There is the palpable knowledge of how difficult and lonely this is for our loved ones. The disruption of normal caregiving activities is definitely painfully felt on both sides of the equation. From time to time, there are also other situations, usually involving sickness, in which barriers arise for us as caregivers.

When the barriers are beyond our control, there is no choice but to work on letting go of what we cannot change. There is a sadness to the situation, yes, and it deserves to be felt and expressed. But we can also let it lead to acceptance. There is a lot to be said for doing the best we can with the situation given to us. Our loved ones have already survived much; this is a chance for them to remember their own resilience.

*When events beyond my control interfere with how I give care, I can feel sadness, work towards acceptance, and resolve to do the best I can do for today's situation.*

## *March 11*

***"It's always the mind that needs quieting and the heart that needs listening to."***

—Rasheed Ogunlaru

The emergency phone calls from my mother's facility or from my sister almost always set off sensations of feeling overwhelmed. There were a wide range of falls, bouts of flu, sometimes a concern between Mom and the staff. Like an ocean tide, the waves of concern just seemed to be a regular part of the process. But also like the tide, there were ways to follow the crest of the crisis with an ebbing away of anxiety.

Whatever the fire was, we found a way to put it out. When extra hands were needed, they were found. Every time a crisis hit, one of the most helpful things for me was to take a few deep breaths, to prioritize what needed to happen and what I needed to rearrange. It is truly a heart journey—our hearts guide us to make the right choice in any situation. There is a stillness in our hearts where we can always find calm.

*As a crisis crests like a wave, we can always find a way to quietly ebb our sense of being overwhelmed. In its place, our hearts will find calm and clarity.*

## *March 12*

***"Whoever you are, no matter how lonely,***
***the world offers itself to your imagination,***
***calls to you like the wild geese, harsh and exciting—***
***over and over announcing your place***
***in the family of things."***

—Mary Oliver, *Wild Geese*

Feelings of loneliness are familiar to most humans, and at times as a caregiver that loneliness will come upon us. Even with a good support system, there will be those moments when we feel alone with a huge responsibility or alone as powerful feelings wash over and through us.

Yet the world offers us many gifts and invites our imaginations to reach out at such times. There is endless potential for an image in the world to touch us in some way, to give us pause. It may be the wild geese flying beautifully overhead, the autumn leaves turning into glorious shades, the tiny bud emerging, or the green splendor of a hillside in spring or summer. Over and over again, we are invited to know that we have a unique and beloved place inside of all this vibrant life around us.

*When I come upon lonely moments as a caregiver,*
*I can look for how the world around me invites*
*me to a wide and wondrous sense of belonging.*

## *March 13*

***"Blessed are they who make it known***
***That I'm loved, respected and not alone."***

—Esther Mary Walker, *Beatitudes for Friends of the Aged*

Beatitudes are blessings—originally delivered by Jesus, according to the Gospel of Mark—but they have been adapted in beautiful ways over time. This adaptation is specifically for friends of the those who are aged or vulnerable in some other way. In two short lines, the writer underscores the basic important principles of caregiving: our purpose is one of love, a love that embodies respect for our loved one and a companionship which lets them know they are not alone on this trail.

Furthermore, these lines invoke blessings for those who provide this kind of love and companionship. As we invest our time and energy, it is helpful to know that our efforts are appreciated and even being blessed—sometimes by people we don't even know. To be blessed is to have a special light shone upon us.

*May the blessings around me quietly illuminate the love, respect, and companionship that are the best of me as a caregiver.*

## March 14

***"That's the wonderful way life works; we pay forward kindnesses shown to us, and we offer love as we would want to be loved. That is the renewing source of spiritual strength for any of us."***

—Rev. Dr. Paul C. Hayes

This quote captures the essence, or one of the essences, of what caregiving is really about. Most of us have been the beneficiaries of many kindnesses in our lives. Most of us were raised by caring parents. As caregivers, we are simply passing on what has been given to us. Ideally, we are loving another the way we ourselves would choose to be loved if we were the vulnerable one—which we probably will be at some other time.

There is a renewal in this awareness of the circle of care. We have received care, so we give care and hope to receive it ourselves when in need. We are part of the larger circle of life. At times it may seem like you are alone, so it helps to consciously remember this circle. It helps to remember how important caregiving is to keep that circle going.

*Today I will honor the part I play in the caregiving circle—it is truly a cycle of life and love.*

## *March 15*

***"The principle of compassion lies at the heart of all religious, ethical and spiritual traditions, calling us always to treat all others as we wish to be treated ourselves."***

—From *The International Charter for Compassion*

Religious and secular leaders and philosophers from all over the world put together the above Charter, and this is a small but emblematic part of it. The charter is designed to make the world a better place, to provide a template for humanitarian ideals. It is worth pausing over, as a caregiver, to think of how we ourselves would want to be treated if we woke up tomorrow terminally sick, unable to walk, or disoriented and forgetful beyond recognition.

Wouldn't we want to know we are still loved and valued? Wouldn't we prefer gentle and loving expressions of care to a hurried and impatient sense of duty? Yes and yes. These ideals stated above are taken into consideration when peace prizes are awarded. They are noble ideals and ones that we as caregivers are challenged to reach for on an almost daily basis. It is not an award-winning job, this job of caregiving. But it should be.

*Today I will remember how important it is to be with my loved one and do things for my loved one from a place of compassion. Whatever my spiritual belief, this is an opportunity to grow and deepen on my own spiritual path.*

## *March 16*

***"You can't use up creativity. The more you use, the more you have."***

—Maya Angelou

It is helpful as a caregiver to be creative about ways to interact with your loved one. My dad loved music, so sometimes I could take him down to the communal piano where I played and he sang or would happily listen. This was fun and a great break from routine for both of us. A good friend of mine likes to play cards with his father. They often save that for Saturday afternoons.

We kept photo albums handy, so when grandchildren came to visit, this was an easy and fun way to spend time together. Everyone enjoys looking back at milestones and at themselves at younger ages. Watching movies together, especially all-time favorites, can be a great way to spend time together in an easygoing and casual way.

*Shared activities can be fun for both caregiver and loved one. My creativity is ongoing: as needs change, I can continue to find ways to make our time together fun and meaningful.*

## *March 17*

***"You'll come and find the place where I am lying And kneel and say an Ave there for me."***

—"Danny Boy" by Fred Weatherly

This well-known Irish song is known to bring tears to the eyes of many people—whether listening to it or singing it. An annual event at a church near my home features this song sung from the altar every year on the Sunday nearest St. Patrick's Day. People gather around, for its beauty and for the way it acknowledges a future death but in the present tense. I am always struck by people wiping their eyes, heads bowed or soaking it up in a deeply thoughtful way. This need to honor death when one sees it coming, or when it has passed through a loved one, is a powerful and universal need. And goodbyes are always so hard.

In some ways, caregiving is an extended goodbye. Yes, there is the focus on the moment, the appreciation of each day's journey. But for most caregivers, we know what the end result is that we are trying to work toward as gracefully as we possibly can. Having a cathartic moment here or there about this is an important acknowledgment of our path and of the road our loved one is on. Finding some solace for this aspect of our journey is healing—whether it comes through music or just through time to reflect upon and honor the long goodbye we are living.

*In the midst of my busy life, I can take the time to find solace for the sadness that is part of watching my loved one suffer and move toward his or her final days. Solace is all around me— it's a matter of reaching for it.*

## *March 18*

***"Love is the key we must turn***
***Truth is the flame we must burn***
***. . .***
***Do you know what I mean?***
***Have your eyes really seen?"***

—"Love Song" by Lesley Duncan (sung by Elton John)

Love and truth are certainly part of this journey as caregivers. Sometimes difficult truths need to be shared; doing so with an attitude of love can make all the difference in the world. Even as we open the door to our loved one's room, we can envision ourselves turning the key of love. The world is a busy place and demands of us many complicated roles and chores. It is so easy to get caught up in the many demands of our lives.

These words help us distill the truth. When we are seeing clearly, with mind and heart, we see living each day in a loving way is really what is important. We see how important it is to be truthful, even—and especially with—ourselves. Meaning is to be found in the path of truth and love, and caregiving gives us ample opportunity to practice this.

*Today I will pause and consider how love is the key I am turning every day as a caregiver. I will see it clearly for what it is: a gift.*

## March 19

***"The little things? The little moments? They aren't little."***

—Jon Kabat-Zinn

Caregiving sounds like one cohesive "thing": a job? A role? Yet in actuality, it is a way of thinking and being that is expressed in the world as many small moments and small fleeting gestures. The worth of this journey can be underscored and understood when we remember and honor how much those little moments matter—both to ourselves and to our loved one.

The phone call, the card in the mail, the smile on your face as you enter the room your loved one spends a lot of time in: all gestures of love that matter. The sharing of the small treat you brought with you, the writing of cards when your loved one no longer can: more gestures of love. Your picking up the new round of medication at the drugstore, the genuine expression of appreciation: all gestures of love. From Kabat-Zinn, teacher and mentor to many on the power of mindfulness, comes the reminder that the small moments carry deep meaning.

*Today I will remember that my small gestures as a caregiver are meaningful; they matter to me and to my loved one and help make the world a kinder and gentler place.*

## *March 20*

***"The spring equinox represents new light and life, new beginnings, seeds, and paths."***

—Google

Spring equinox happens when the hours of light and dark are almost equally balanced. Although the actual date is not set in stone, it is usually close to the 20th of March. Honored throughout all time, it has been documented and studied by even the earliest astrologers. It also happens to be within close range to many important religious holidays: Passover, Easter, and more.

This need to reach for the light is both deeply human and deeply connected to the rhythms and cycles of nature. Light always returns, and this is true cause for celebration. That is why, for centuries, this time of year is honored and celebrated in large and quiet ways. On our paths as caregivers, we can notice and enjoy the extra minutes of daylight that come our way each day. We can feel touched by the hope that light carries. Whatever our struggles are, our energy is being deeply renewed by this time of year. As the quiet seeds gather strength to blossom, so too does our love energy—seasonally and even daily—renew itself for the blossoming ahead.

*The rhythms at work in nature remind me that light always returns. No matter what kind of day I am having, I can look for and celebrate how this time of year renews me.*

## *March 21*

***"I don't regret anything I've ever done in life, any choice that I've made. But I'm consumed with regret for the things I didn't do, the choices I didn't make, the things I didn't say . . . "***

—Trevor Noah

Caregiving is an opportunity to "pay ahead," an opportunity to express thanks for what we have received in the past, and above all, to be there for our loved one in ways that, if omitted, we would surely regret at a later time. Hard as it might be to find the time for these gestures in the here and now, every small gesture builds a cornucopia of love. Any way that we have to let go of our burdens, if only for the time we spend with our loved one today, all the better.

For gestures of love are most authentic and effective when they come from that deep well of care that we all have inside of us—which sometimes gets obscured by fatigue or a particularly hard day. "How will we feel about today's action tomorrow?" is a question often worth asking, even through a cloud of fatigue. That is one way to move into the deeper well of our values.

*My choices today as a human being and as a caregiver can fruitfully be measured by what I don't want to regret tomorrow.*

## *March 22*

***"Music acts like a magic key, to which the most tightly closed heart opens."***

—Maria von Trapp

My friend Jenny's father was going through a difficult time. He had just been moved to a memory unit, the change was hard, and he was being obstinate and crabby. Among other problems, the TV in the new place wasn't working right. Jenny was starting to receive calls from the nursing staff about what to do. Her brother saved the day in a couple of ways. First, he and Jenny brainstormed: what had their father loved all of his life? Musicals. He could sing every word to most songs from "Singing in the Rain" to "The Sound of Music" to "Oliver!."

Jenny's brother set up the TV with a VCR and brought in his stash of old-fashioned DVDs. He showed his father how to put in a movie and wrote down the instructions. It took some cajoling, but within a few days even the staff began to notice that their father was calmer. And when he did get upset, they could often settle him down by taking care of the needs at hand and then setting him up with one of his movies. As Jen, her brother, or an aide walked out of the room, they could hear him humming along to what he was watching.

*When your loved one's heart has been tightened by difficulties, sometimes music will reopen that heart in simple and surprising ways.*

## *March 23*

***"It is you who became yourself***
***But those before you***
***Are a part of your fabric."***

—rupi kaur

The path of caregiving is one that is underscored by remembering we are the recipients of those who have come before us. We are, all of us, imbued with strengths and generosities that have been shared and passed down. Often, we have learned from what was lacking. Sometimes, when the path felt hard, I remembered my immigrant great grandparents and how hard they worked to carve out a life, having crossed the ocean and landed in Canadian wilderness.

Sometimes when the path felt hard, I remembered my Aunt Gert, who was an extended family caregiver. She always did so with warmth in her heart and boundless empathy for anyone around her who was suffering. She was quick to smile, dance, and laugh as well. On my tired days, I would think of her and feel her presence lifting my heart for the day's tasks.

*Part of the fabric of my life comes from those who went before me; I remember their wisdom as a way to feel blessed and energized for this day.*

## *March 24*

**"Caregiving often calls us to lean into love we didn't know possible."**

—Tia Walker

I think none of us really know how we will respond in the trenches until we are there. Some of us have perhaps always expressed a caring way in the world. But for others of us, reaching out to care might be more unexpected, or even a new way of being. We may have a broad range of feelings toward and about the person for whom we are providing care.

A friend of mine spoke of the things she was learning about her Dad, who she had been estranged from during an earlier time in their relationship. One day, they emptied a drawer together, and she asked gentle questions about things he had saved: a letter from her, some of his war-time medals. At times, both had tears in their eyes. Her mother had already passed on, and she was the family member who was closest in proximity. What surprised her was the way her love for her father was opening in unexpected and deep ways.

*As caregivers we cannot create such moments, but we can rest assured that the potential for deepening love is an integral part of this path. Like alert birdwatchers, we can look and listen for the golden moments.*

## *March 25*

***"A little bit of mercy makes the world less cold and more just."***

—Pope Francis

In many Christian services, there is a section where the participants ask for mercy and then ask to be granted peace. I am always moved by the words and the melody that accompanies this part of the service. Who among us doesn't need or desire mercy from time to time? Mercy is defined as kindness and compassion; every word that captures these important qualities enriches our communal vocabulary.

Mercy reminds me of the Leonard Cohen song titled "Sisters of Mercy"; it is one of my favorites. I often thought, during our caregiving years, of my sisters and I as the sisters of mercy. This both touched and amused me and gave me a worthy soundtrack for my experience. But the truth is that as much as I felt my caregiving job was to deliver mercy, to show up in a kind and compassionate way, I also needed mercy every step of the way.

*May the giving and receiving of mercy make my world warmer and more peaceful today.*

## *March 26*

***"Whenever your mind becomes scattered, use your breath as the means to take hold of your mind again."***

—Thich Nhat Hanh

Due to the high incidence of crisis during anyone's time of caregiving, it is easy to fall into the "fight or flight" mentality. It's a very human response; in fact, we are hard-wired for it. But often our best thinking does not come from this stance, and it is hard on our bodies to spend too much in fight or flight mode. Thus, we need ways to calm ourselves down, ways to carve out a more centered way of responding to the needs at hand.

Breath is a key here. Focusing on slowing down our breathing or taking a few deep breaths will counteract the urge of our bodies to react out of adrenaline. One doesn't need to be an experienced yoga master to utilize the tool of slowing down our fear responses through concentrated breathing. This simple tool is accessible to all. Focused breathing taps us into a more centered and more heartfelt connection to our spirits.

*No matter what is happening around me, I can let the small simple wind of my breath calm my spirit today.*

## *March 27*

***"Relationships never end; they just change. In believing that lies the freedom to carry compassion, empathy, love, kindness and respect into and through whatever changes. We are made more by that practice."***

—Richard Wagamese

In the caregiving realm, there are often a lot of relationship and role changes. Someone once strong is now dealing with daily vulnerabilities. Perhaps that sharp and capable person you once knew is compromised either memory-wise or physically. Stepping in to help might not be a role you ever imagined, but here it is. At times it feels like we have lost what once was, and in some ways, this is true.

But the stronger truth is that the connection has lived through time. The ongoing thread is the relationship, the interwoven tapestry created between human beings. We honor that by facing the changes with compassion, respect, and kindness. And while we do it to meet a need in another person, doing so deepens and expands who we are.

*Change challenges me to crawl inside the word compassion. I will let compassion for my loved one, and for myself, carry me today.*

## *March 28*

***"There is a time to weep, and a time to laugh . . . "***

—Ecclesiastes 3

So often in a caregiving relationship, what is most important is the ability to discern what our loved one most needs on any given day. Perhaps it is also about discerning what we need. Is it a day to honor and embrace the sadness and to share the tears? Is it a day to acknowledge the simple gifts of love and life and celebrate through laughter and joy?

Wide ranges of emotions are touched as we share a journey like this with a loved one. This line from its much longer, beautiful passage reminds us there is a time to weep and a time to laugh. It is most important to recognize, honor, and embrace the timing for whatever expression is most authentically ours today.

*Both tears and laughter have their place on my journey; let me honor what is coming to the surface for today.*

## *March 29*

***"Above all, trust in the slow work of God. . . . it is the law of all progress that it may take a very long time."***

—Pierre Teilhard de Chardin

Movement in the world of caregiving can seem very slow at times. Although often punctuated by crises, there are many weeks or months of slow progress or of the situation coming slowly into a greater clarity. The need for patience cannot be underestimated. The ability to practice patience is connected to a belief that what is happening for our loved one and for us is largely in the hands of a higher power, a benevolent force in the universe, a God by whatever name you are most comfortable using. Perhaps at its deepest and most essential level, this power is pure love.

When anxiety or worry or frustration surface, as they so often do, we can listen to the words of this Jesuit priest who was also a paleontologist and a geologist. He clearly studied the world, in many of its forms. Layers of rocks are slow to reveal change; the history of animal species on our planet is full of slow changes over time. On this caregiving journey, when progress feels slow, we can recognize that we are a small part of an ancient and timeless rhythm.

*Forces larger than myself are at work; as I choose to trust a wisdom that is beyond me, I will find patience and peace.*

## *March 30*

***"Blessed are they who know the ways***
***To bring back memories of yesterdays."***

—Esther Mary Walker, *Beatitudes for Friends of the Aged*

Both storytelling and going through old photos are great ways to allow someone to step back into memories of an easier time. In fact, photos are a great entry point for asking questions. There is no need for a lot of photos, just a few can spark questions. And questions are so often the beginning point of stories.

My friend told me of spending such a pleasant afternoon with her father, going through one small picture album from a holiday gathering decades before. Her father knew who everyone was, remembered interesting details from the meal and celebration. He kept talking about what a beautiful day that was, how special it felt then—special enough he could still feel it, decades later.

*It is a gift to shine the light on a fully lived life through time spent sharing photo albums and stories. I will find time for that soon to lift up my heart and my loved one's.*

## *March 31*

**"Love is the beauty of the soul."**

—St. Augustine

There are so many kinds of beauty in this world, and the awareness and appreciation of beauty almost always uplifts us. I remember noticing how beautiful my mother's face was in certain moments, and I was struck that beauty can be seen in a 95-year-old face. Sometimes a beautiful fresh flower gave us reason to pause and feel the full force of its special texture, color, and scent. There were unexpected and beautiful moments.

One of my favorite beautiful moments took place when my daughter accompanied me one day when my mom, her grandmother, was in a rehab facility. It was no one's favorite place, and we were all grateful it was temporary. Entering that hard place was easier for me with my daughter at my side. When we arrived, Mom asked for her back to be rubbed. Usually I did so, but this day my daughter stepped in. As her grandmother "Ooh"-ed and "Aah"-ed with the relief she felt from a simple back rub, she told us how she prays for all of us all of the time. Tears flowed down my daughter's face and my own as the power of loving touch transformed my mother's day and the force of her life filled the room with a special light.

*One way to uplift and sustain myself on this journey is to honor the moments of beauty that happen and allow them to fully enter and energize me.*

# April

## *April 1*

***"Rhymes for April—let me sing***
***The pleasures of returning spring...***
***Fools are made, by far the worst***
***On other days besides the First."***

—"April Rhymes," *The Comic Almanack for 1835*

Although the exact origins of April Fools' Day are unknown, it has been celebrated for centuries in multiple cultures. Pranks, hoaxes, and bait-and-switch surprises are all intended to ultimately lighten up the day of those at the receiving end when they finally hear the words "April Fools'!"

It's a chance to switch things up and have some fun. A friend of mine went to the window of the living room at his father's place and gasped, "Dad, there's a bear in your yard!" (This can be easily replaced with any animal that is unlikely but not too farfetched.) He had arranged for his children to be outside the window at that moment. As his dad hobbled over to check out the bear, they raised their signs that shouted out April Fools'! The surprise was multiple—no grandchildren were expected that day, so that was the best wonderful surprise, delivered in a way that marked the day as a special one.

*We can all use April Fools' Day as a chance to lighten things up for ourselves and our loved ones. There's a very good reason it has been celebrated for centuries all over the world—we all need reminders to take life less seriously, at least for today.*

## *April 2*

**"Help us to communicate rather than compete."**

*—Prayer for the Whole Human Family*

Sometimes when you are part of a caregiver team, especially if you are siblings, there can be elements of competition. Even though your adult brain knows it is a waste of energy, you might find yourself noticing who does more or less in different areas of caregiving. Sometimes the stress of the job brings out the worst in each of us. But other times we are just in need of credit for what we do.

When caregiving feels competitive, something is out of balance, and often communication is key. One must communicate clearly with oneself first of all: if I am feeling competitive, what is it that I need to do differently? Then communicating that need, to oneself and to other members of one's team, is vitally important. We are not on opposing sides; we share the same goal.

*When we find ourselves in the lose-lose mindset of comparing and competing, it is time to take a clear look at our needs and communicate them.*

## *April 3*

***"Passover is a celebration of spring, of birth and rebirth, of a journey from slavery to freedom, and of taking responsibility for yourself, the community, and the world. . . . "***

—History.com

Based deep in the history of the Jews' exodus out of slavery in ancient Egypt, Passover is celebrated by Jews in the early spring. Its focus on rebirth and spring echoes the Christian holiday of Easter, which is celebrated around the same time. Passover is celebrated over a period of seven days in honor of the days of their journey out of Egypt. Special foods, ritual storytelling, and gathering together are all integral parts of this ritual.

In the caregiving world, honoring traditions like this can underscore the meaning of our time together. If you and/or your caregiver have grown up inside such a rich tradition, then honoring it in even small and simple ways can lift you both. Even those who have lost appetite might rise to celebrate a special food, a candlelit moment, an immersion into history. Especially poignant is the realization that our time together to celebrate is finite.

*On special days, the richness of tradition, as we take time to honor it, can infuse our time together in deeply meaningful ways.*

## *April 4*

***"Easter is a Christian holiday that celebrates the belief in the resurrection of Jesus Christ. . . . Although a holiday of high religious significance in the Christian faith, many traditions associated with Easter date back to pre-Christian, pagan times. . . . "***

—History.com

Although based in its own unique Christian heritage, Easter celebrates the renewal of the human spirit that has been part of spring celebrations across a wide swath of time and places. It is closely aligned—in date and in what it essentially honors—with the Jewish Passover. Easter is celebrated around the same time that pagans, long before Christianity arrived, celebrated the abundance of gifts of new life in this time of year.

My mother had celebrated Easter all of her life, but her last Easter, just weeks before she died, was a simple and sacred one. My husband, daughter, son-in-law, and I spent the afternoon with her. There was a quiet light in her room, and we brought her then-current favorite food treat: a caramel sundae. In my lifetime, I have yet to see someone so enjoy that simple treat, savoring each bit, savoring our companionship. And we savored hers, her intense awareness of the pleasure and gift of this moment. Although she was journeying toward death, resurrection and rebirth and the bounty of spring still touched her—and all of us—deeply.

*In the way that best suits my loved one, we can share the energy of Easter and spring and let it infuse us with a deeper, fresher energy and sense of meaning today.*

## *April 5*

***"Perhaps the most 'spiritual' thing any of us can do is simply to look through our own eyes, see with eyes of wholeness, and act with integrity and kindness."***

—Jon Kabat-Zinn

During the time I was actively caregiving, I was also seeing a spiritual advisor. This was enormously helpful, for I had and have a propensity to see my spiritual life as separate from other parts of my life. She always helped guide me back to many aspects of my life, but especially what I was doing as a caregiver. Seeing with eyes of wholeness included seeing my mother, not just for who she had been at many different stages of our lives, but who she was as a woman growing old in her body, living alone after decades of a long marriage.

One night I dreamt of hugging her, and both of us had tears in our eyes. I awoke realizing that above all, we were two women, growing older together in this shared life on planet earth. This dream helped melt some of the differences I felt between us. The dream, my advisor's wise counsel, and each day helped me to feel the fullness of integrity in our relationship and to know that genuine kindness mattered.

*Approaching our caregiving days with integrity and kindness both nourishes and is an expression of our spiritual lives.*

## *April 6*

***"Feelings come and go like clouds in a windy sky. Conscious breathing is my anchor."***

—Thich Nhat Hahn

So many emotions get tapped throughout our days as caregivers. There are many ups and downs, steps forward then backward. Feelings of hope can be quickly followed by feelings of disappointment. There may be days of calm followed by anxiety and fear. One plan feels settled, and just as you are adjusting to it, the situation changes and you are caught off-guard, unsure what to do next.

In the Buddhist tradition of meditation, practitioners focus on observing their feelings and not getting too attached to any of them. This sounds much simpler than it is. The ideal is to keep finding one's center and hopefully a calm center, no matter what the ups and downs are, no matter the feelings that are currently being stirred. The beautiful image of feelings as clouds is so helpful. Clouds have many moods, and they are always moving and transforming. There is always a natural beauty to them. So, too, there is a beauty to our feelings, for they are expressions of our care.

*A wide range of feelings is part of our daily lives as caregivers; we can cherish the variety of clouds in our sky and keep returning to our center, our breath.*

## April 7

***"We ourselves feel that what we are doing is just a drop in the ocean. But the ocean would be less because of that missing drop."***

—Mother Teresa

Often in my caregiving days, I felt that what I was able to do was a small drop in the ocean of need. The days I felt most discouraged were the days it felt like I was up against a bottomless well of need. There were many factors which created this perception, some of them having to do with my own vulnerabilities, some with my mother's, and some just with the intense and ongoing nature of giving care to someone who is becoming more and more frail.

Yet here is a reminder—from a holy woman who made such a difference in so many lives—that each person's drop in the ocean matters. Perhaps this way of thinking was a huge part of Mother Teresa's ability to care so much and accomplish so greatly. A gesture as small as a phone call or as large as a day spent with your loved one—it all matters and makes a difference.

*My small drop matters in the ocean of love;*
*for today, that is more than enough.*

## *April 8*

**"Compassion becomes real when we recognize our shared humanity."**

—Pema Chodron

We all have much in common when it comes to the big things in life. Physical pain is difficult for all of us. To one degree or another, many of us fear and question how we will approach death. We all ache when things go wrong for our loved ones, and goodbyes stretch our hearts in bittersweet ways. When we know our heart's place with such things, with pain and heartache and loss, then we are much more able to enter into caregiving in a compassionate way.

We are all part of a huge mystery; no one fully knows its secrets or answers. Pursuing the mystery, exploring it, and living it is part of what life on earth is all about. This is a powerful path to share, and caregiving becomes a very special way to share this mystery with our loved one. The pain, the unanswered questions, the love embedded in bittersweet goodbyes—all are part of our shared humanity.

*I am grateful today for the compassion I feel when I am aware of our shared humanity—with all people but especially with our loved ones.*

## *April 9*

***"If you should feel stalled, numb, or exhausted from the trials of your life, simply slow . . . your heart to the pace of the earth soaking up rain, and wait for the freshness of the beginning to greet you."***

—Mark Nepo

In many caregiving situations, the needs are daily and, in a crisis, hourly. It is only human to feel tired; it is only human to feel worn out by continuous needs. There is often an emotional toll as well as a physical one; it is so hard to watch a loved one suffer. A wide range of moods in a vulnerable person will challenge even the most patient of caregivers. For all these reasons, exhaustion is part of the journey. And it is usually the signal that you need an afternoon off or a day away. Or, that it is time to draw on and reach out to your support team.

Often even a short break can help re-energize you. A break entails a time to slow down, perhaps to slow the mind and spirit as much as anything. Such slowing down can help bring us back to the source, to the core impulse embedded in this role. Relief can be found in taking time for coffee with a friend who understands what you are going through. Or taking a long slow walk in a favorite place of nature; nature can calm us in explicably important ways.

*Today I will take the time to re-energize in a way that works for me—a healing break will help me realign with the source of my caregiving energy.*

## *April 10*

***"It is one of the beautiful compensations of this life that no one can sincerely help another without helping himself."***

—Charles Dudley Warner

During photosynthesis in green plants, light energy is captured and used to convert water, carbon dioxide, and minerals into oxygen and energy-rich organic compounds. Without photosynthesis, we don't have enough oxygen to breathe. Without photosynthesis, plants don't grow, and we don't have food. Sunlight shines on leaves; the leaves soak it up, transform it, and give back to the world in a variety of forms—mostly through food and breath.

One could liken caregiving to shining light on our loved one: the light of attention. That attention, in turn, is absorbed and returned in ways that nourish us deeply. Food and breath. The moments of tenderness with a loved one, the moments of glimpsing deep into both the past and the future, or eternity, are the gifts of exchange for a caregiver.

*Today I will notice the ways that caregiving is deeply enriching my life.*

## *April 11*

***"If we approach the act of caring as though we are giving something to someone who is weaker than ourselves, we will never relate to another as a whole person."***

—Kirsten DeLeo

The healthiest and most soul-satisfying avenue for being a caregiver embodies a deep respect for your loved one. Yes, maybe he or she is unable to walk in the moment or maybe they have forgotten so much of what they used to know, but inside of their heart live all of their previous selves. Your care honors not just who they are today but who they have been in their lifetime; your care honors the gifts you yourself have received from them over time.

This is particularly challenging for family members caring for loved ones with memory loss. It's disorienting, especially if they don't recognize or specifically respond to you, their caregiver. I overheard a nurse say that even in such circumstances, somewhere deep in that loved one's heart, your voice and presence is recognized. Your presence brings a familiar comfort—even if your loved one has lost the ability to respond.

*No matter the wide range of responses from my loved one, I will remember that I show up to honor who she or he has been in their lifetime and, in particular, in my life. I honor their whole person, and in doing so, I acknowledge my whole history.*

## *April 12*

***"When the month of Ramadan arrives, the doors of mercy are opened."***

—Sahih Muslim

One evening in early April, I was walking around the city lake near my home. Tucked behind a parked van were two men on prayer mats, heads bowed down to the ground in evening prayer. They faced the direction of the soon-to-be setting sun. They were just slightly off the beaten track, yet all around them zoomed bikes and cars and people walking and talking.

I was moved by their quiet focus, by the peacefulness they exuded, by their quiet but open practice of their faith. Just seeing them made me feel more reverent toward the evening, the sun making its way across the lake and through the just barely budding trees. My Muslim friend reminds me that Ramadan is a month for mercy, for forgiveness, for blessings. Who among us doesn't need more of all of those? Inside the busyness of caregiving, there are many reminders all around us of our shared human need for mercy. That is one of the beauties of our wider world.

*In the midst of our days of caregiving, let us remember to seek the blessing of mercy—
it is a deep human need.*

## *April 13*

***"We provide the best care for our loved ones and for ourselves when we take the time to evaluate the limits of our capabilities. We might have to change our plans, ask for help, or find a compromise."***

—Barry Jacobs and Julia Mayer

Many spiritual and healing practices focus on the dual challenge of learning to love oneself and to love and respect others. Caregiving can and most likely will provide opportunities for an advanced degree in both. There is the dual goal here: how to provide the best care for our loved one and—what is often overlooked—how to provide the best care for ourselves as well. As much as the path of caregiving is one of generosity, of helping someone who is at a vulnerable place, this rugged journey will give rise to our own vulnerabilities. Such vulnerabilities show up in the form of exhaustion or burnout or crabbiness or that moment when you realize something has to change.

It's okay. You get to honor your own journey here as well. A decision that is kind to yourself will make you a better caregiver. Old ways of thinking may tell us it's a choice between self and other; a better approach is to find solutions that make it better for both of you. Such solutions are often found by asking for help and working to find a compromise that benefits all.

*Today I will honor and honestly evaluate my own needs, reflecting on what will help me to care in the best way possible for both myself and my loved one.*

## *April 14*

***"So compassion means to endure with another person, to put ourselves in somebody else's shoes, to feel her pain as though it were our own . . . "***

—Karen Armstrong

All definitions of compassion can be distilled down to the words above, written by an internationally recognized spiritual leader of our times. And, essentially, when you sign on as a caregiver, you are signing up for a crash course on compassion. Let's take this apart: "to put ourselves in somebody else's shoes" means to exert the effort to open one's heart and imagine what it is like for this other person, this loved one. Since illness is random and aging will affect all of us at some point, both are an integral part of the human journey. Most of us have had physical pain or injuries along the way; it is helpful to remember how vulnerable, and perhaps frustrated, we felt in those times. Many of our loved ones, once they need caregiving, are in much more extreme pain and dealing with multiple limitations.

That brings us to "endure with another person." For the most part, we cannot change what is happening. But, as our loved one must endure what is happening in their bodies and brains, there is an opportunity for us to practice deep compassion. To endure with them, doing whatever we can to help him or her feel less alone on this part of their life journey. To show up, to be there—it matters both for them and for ourselves.

*An important aspect of my job as a caregiver is to draw deep from a well of compassion—tuning in to what my loved one is going through and enduring the harder days with as much comfort and grace as possible.*

## *April 15*

***"As I walk, as I walk, the universe is walking with me."***

—From the Navajo rain dance ceremony

As I write this meditation, the rain is softly falling outside every window from which I look out upon the world. As I write this, the world is spinning inside of the crisis of COVID-19. Yet the softness of the day's rain is deeply soothing. Barely thawed grasses and earth absorb the moisture and send out radiant aromas. Wet tree bark deepens into a mysterious beauty. Deep inside the earth, seeds and bulbs are preparing to emerge and energize the world with their green and abundant splendor; we can count on that.

In the meantime, there is a muted energy in the air that is palpable, and what is germinating is still hidden from view. So often, amid days of caregiving, the fruit of our efforts can be hard to see. We may have days where we feel our own muted energy. That is okay, the rainy day reminds us. Quiet, subdued days are part of any journey through this life.

*As I walk this path as a caregiver, the natural world reminds me every day of how to accept life's rhythms.*

## *April 16*

**"Make a list of what is really important to you. Embody it."**

—Jon Kabat-Zinn

Here is such a simple and powerful tool: make a list. By listing what is important to us, we help bring into focus our values. As caregivers, we might have on that list something like being a compassionate person, being a steadfast and loyal partner, or being a loving daughter or son or niece or nephew. Once it is on that list, you have given it credence.

Of course, there will be multiple items on the list. But the aspect of being a caregiver that is most important to you comes into focus when written down. By naming this value, it becomes easier to embrace and to embody it. In a world that loves quantifying things, such a list allows our important ways of being to be named and honored.

*Today I will honor the values on my list of what is important and settle more deeply into being and embodying those values.*

## *April 17*

***"Creativity doesn't wait for that perfect moment. It fashions its own perfect moments out of ordinary ones."***

—Bruce Garrabrandt

My good friend Linda was agonizing over not being able to visit her father in a care facility during the virus outbreak. Sometimes she drove to the facility, stood outside, and waved to her father through the window as they talked on the phone. Wondering what else she might do to make her father's long days less lonely, she felt the spark of an idea. She asked all of her relatives—cousins, siblings, children—to send him a card, all the better if it included a photo of the sender.

The following week, her phone conversation consisted of an upbeat father who had chosen a favorite bowl to hold all the cards he had received. He kept them handy so he could go through them often. When talking on the phone to his loved ones, he often read a card aloud and then described the picture. This caregiver found a creative solution to a problem; the daily trip to the mailbox brightened up his day and brought him gifts he could look at over and over again. The people enlisted to help were happy to do so. She asked for help and received it beyond what she imagined.

*For every dilemma I run into as a caregiver, my well of creativity can help me find a way to make the ordinary moment a better one.*

## *April 18*

***"My job is not to solve people's problems or make them happy, but to help them see the grace operating in their lives."***

—Eugene H. Peterson, *The Contemplative Pastor*

Pastoral care is often available in care facilities and always in hospitals. In his last weeks, my father had a pastor who came regularly to meet with him and pray with him; this was organized through the local hospice program. I always appreciated it when Nick showed up; he inspired a friendly, comforting, and spiritually nuanced conversation. Near the end of his visit, he would ask my Dad if he wanted to pray with him, which Dad always did. And then the blessing he would give—which was full of thanks for my father's full life, his family around him, and prayers for courage for the day and for all that lay ahead—often moved me to tears. Nick was often in and out in less than a half hour, but his presence always provided my Dad and me, and anyone else around, with an extra sense of comfort.

Such resources can also be found through community programs. Also, if your loved one has been part of a religious community, then perhaps there is a pastor, or a trained lay person who would come. It helps take some burden off of the caregiver. Men and women in pastoral care provide an added dimension and, in my experience, do so with a sensitive compassion to vulnerability.

*If pastoral care is available and my loved one is open to it, I can find ways to make that happen for them. It is an incredibly helpful resource.*

## *April 19*

***"To love is to cherish the individual standing before you presently—charms, quirks, and all. To love is to give someone a piece of your heart that you will never, ever reclaim."***

—Richelle E. Goodrich, *Smile Anyway*

When we are caring for a loved one who has changed significantly, this is always a helpful reminder. So often they change in ways that are hard for both them and for those of us who care for them. It is the daily challenge to adapt to who he or she is today rather than who they were ten or thirty years ago.

"Accepting the things we cannot change" is an important line of the Serenity Prayer. The wise words remind us that our primary goal is to give care, not advice or formulas for change. The heart-opening and sometimes heartbreaking path we are on requires us to love and cherish them exactly as they are today. Some days that meant, for me, dealing with anxiety in someone who was always previously capable and in charge. Kindness and gentle reassurance felt like the only possible response. To do so, I had to let go of my desire to fix and change the situation.

*I will let go of the desire to change my loved one and instead accept and cherish my loved one just the way she or he is today.*

## *April 20*

***"Making lives meaningful in old age is new. It therefore requires more imagination and invention than making them merely safe does."***

—Atul Gawande

Imagination and invention are not always the words or concepts that come to mind when one thinks of caregiving. But it is so true that what brings meaning into any individual's life is unique. Although bodily needs must be attended to for basic comfort, it is often the spiritual needs that require a different kind of thinking. What makes this person happy? Is it listening to music, talking to a specific person, doing artwork, walking out in nature? Is it a phone call to an old friend?

In my mother's last weeks, I so wish I would have called my cousin who is a priest. I believe he would have driven the miles to come see her; I believe a blessing from this special nephew would have meant the world to her. I missed it—too busy with the daily crises and my life. It's okay—I created a lot of other kind touches for my mother. But I offer it as an example. Take the time to slow down, perhaps ask your loved one or just brainstorm on your own what would be meaningful. Then do what you can to make it happen.

*Sometimes the best gift is one that comes from my imagination, from thinking outside of the box. I will let my intuition and inventive mind have some space today.*

## April 21

***"Earth and the great weather move me, have carried me away, and move my inward parts with joy."***

—Uvavnuk, Iglulik, 1920

Often caregiving involves being indoors, engaged in multiple details. It is so easy to forget about the wider world, the world of fresh air and ever-changing patterns of wind and beauty. Yet, when we pause to take in that outer world, it can energize us like nothing else. On those days when my mother's energy and the weather aligned and I could take her for a walk, we both felt transformed. At first, she walked beside me, leaning on my arm. Then she used a walker. Then, later, I pushed her in her wheelchair.

No matter the vehicle, the breaths of fresh air, the feeling of a breeze, or sunshine on our faces were always a restorative tonic. I found it remarkable that on the day she died, the weather vacillated between hailstorms and brilliant sun and a powerful wind, as if saying to all of her loved ones, this is a day to pay attention to, a day to be noted. So often the weather accompanies us in ways that speak to us, as if working in concert with us.

*Today I will notice how the natural world expands my sense of connection to my own life force. The natural world can bring joy to me and my loved one in large and small ways.*

## *April 22*

***"The car was my sanctuary . . . with my mother snug in bed, I slumped over the steering wheel, sobbing. Across America . . . middle-aged daughters do this all the time. I never noticed until I became one of them."***

—Jane Gross

In studies about grief, it is acknowledged that one grief can trigger previous griefs. There is a cumulative effect to grief. The bucket fills up and sometimes just needs to spill over in the expression of tears. What we often don't take enough time to acknowledge (because time is short, right?) is the layering of grief and loss that is a part of the caregiver's journey. You are watching your loved one's losses, and of course you are feeling that. Their losses become your losses as well.

Just acknowledging this is helpful and healing. What is harder is to not acknowledge—to have to pretend, to hold onto some former way of being. So when the tears well up inside of you, understand it is your body's wisdom. Your body is reminding you that it's okay to cry, that the situation you are living inside of is full of losses. Name them, shed tears for them, honor them. Loss is integral to love. And a good cry allows all of us to feel a bit cleansed and relieved.

*Today or when the opportunity arises, I will honor the sadness that seems to be part and parcel of this journey. Deep feelings long for the light of expression.*

## *April 23*

***"At each bump on the road there are always decisions to make . . . I felt the full responsibility of being their Advocate. I prayed I made the right choice."***

—Caroline Johnson

Caregiving is rife with dualities. Burden and joy are opposite ends of a shared teeter-totter. So are hope and despair. Part of the burden is the decision-making that so often comes with the territory. There can be many turning points along the way—times when our loved one clearly needs more or a different kind of care, medication decisions, when a doctor's opinion is needed, when some kind of care is no longer working.

Advocating for the needs of our loved one is a big part of our job. It is a lot of responsibility to shoulder. If you have even one person in your life who understands the immense responsibility on your shoulders, it is helpful. And it is even more helpful to have more than one person supporting you, encouraging you, and affirming you. Research is important, as well as looking into available resources. Decisions that are well-informed and made thoughtfully, intentionally, and with the goal of providing safety and comfort for your loved ones eventually become clear. Once made, we can only hope and pray they are the right ones.

*Whatever your spiritual beliefs are, there is a higher power available to you as you make and accept the needed decisions right now.*

## *April 24*

***"When I was a child, the lessons my father taught me had been about perseverance. . . . As an adult watching him in his final years, I also saw how to come to terms with limits that couldn't simply be wished away."***

—Atul Gawande

I still have vivid memories of my frail 94-year-old mother in rehab learning to put weight again on her injured hip and pelvis. Oh, she worked hard. If she regained enough strength, she could return to her home in the assisted living facility she had been in for years. After a couple of weeks, she was able to bear weight and push her walker. I had watched her fight for it every day through pain and discomfort. It was a triumph for her.

But months later, with too many things going wrong, she needed a different mode for coping. As she grappled with loss of mobility and a weaker immune system, she qualified for hospice care. For many, this is a turning point from fighting to accepting. The powerful winds of effort become quiet breezes of relief. I am sure that when my turn comes, I will remember her gracefulness under pressure.

*As I accompany my loved one through changing times, I can enter that same river of courage, of accepting what cannot be changed and making the best of what remains.*

## *April 25*

***"Learn the alchemy***
***True human beings know.***
***The moment you accept***
***What troubles you've been given,***
***The door will open."***

—Rumi

So many times along the journey, with not only my mother but my father and beloved aunts and uncle as well, one or the other or both of us were going through the "oh no" stage. Oh no to the news of another fall, oh no to the arrival of a flu virus, oh no to the latest diagnosis. It's only human, that impulse to wish away or ward off the bad news. But staying in that place of "oh no" for too long is just not helpful.

A mixture of beliefs and common sense allows us to move on, to accept that hard-edged new reality and begin to work with it. There is an alchemy to this process, this filtering through emotions until one arrives at a place of acceptance. The next doors that need to open are waiting there, on the other side of acceptance.

*Today I will sift through my own personal alchemy until I can honor and accept what is. It's the only way to find the next open door.*

## *April 26*

***"You can be a melting snowflake, a drifting leaf,***
***or a nature spirit dancing in a pond.***
***And if you touch any heart with what you do***
***For the brief moments you are here,***
***That is enough."***

—Tosha Silver

We all get to make our choices, right? And for most of us, the choice to be a caregiver is all about our heart. It's about the love we feel for our loved one. It's about feeling called to be a source of love for that person and really, for ourselves as well. For some of us, it is a chance to redeem earlier missed opportunities to express care. Some of us feel called because no one else can do it and we can't bear the thought of this friend or family member not having someone they can count on and turn to for help.

That life is fleeting is an old cliché, in part because it is so true. There are moments when time seems to fly but also when it seems to crawl. Yet overall, the days and weeks and years do tend to speed by. In some ways, our time on earth is as fleeting as a melting snowflake and as full of dance as a drifting leaf. Along the way, how we warm our own hearts by reaching out and touching another's heart is all that matters.

*When I step outside of the demands of ambition,*
*I can truly feel how important this heart-opening*
*journey is, the path of caregiving, of sharing*
*time and space with my loved one.*

## *April 27*

***"Compassion is not a relationship between the healer and the wounded. It's a covenant between equals."***

—Gregory Boyle

All along, we are learning as caregivers, not just by what we give but also by what we receive. Give and take here on this journey is part of what keeps us able to stay in for the long haul. On the rare occasions that my mother opened up and gave me her honest perspective on parts of our shared lives, it was like clouds had lifted above my head. Oh, now that makes sense, I would think to myself, as she confirmed a feeling or suspicion I had. She was more willing to share her true self, and there wasn't much bitterness left in her.

So, not often but once in a while, our time together shed light on parts of my life that had been hidden away, closeted. Yes, I was running errands for her, communicating with the people who took care of her medical needs, organizing care for her with my sister. But she was quietly, occasionally, sharing with me the gifts of her wisdom and of her particular vantage point in our shared history.

*It's important to remember that give and take, over long periods of time, make equal the sharing between my loved one and I. We are in this together, as a team.*

## *April 28*

***"Like the rainbow***
***After the rain***
***Joy will reveal itself***
***After sorrow."***

—rupi kaur

For those struggling with physical, emotional, or cognitive limitations, there is much to which they are saying goodbye. Goodbyes are full of sorrow. As we travel with our loved ones on this path, we of course feel a kindred sorrow. It is a heart-full challenge to witness and be with the sorrows of this journey. Yet as the saying goes, a sorrow shared is halved. As they are too much to bear alone, we help each other carry the sorrows that are a part of life.

And into the sorrow comes the moments of joy, of heart-lifting love and gratitude. For the heart that feels sorrow is also open to joy. And as the second half of that familiar saying states, a joy shared is doubled. Yes, it's a bit of an emotional roller coaster, but the essential and elemental trail we caregivers share with our loved ones is full of both sorrow and joy. This richness is as gorgeous and miraculous as the appearance of rainbows in the sky.

*If there is a dark cloud on my horizon, I can trust that the rainbow will emerge. I embrace the clouds of sorrow and the many beautiful hues of joy.*

## *April 29*

***"Ramadan is like the Rain. It nourishes the seed of good deeds."***

—Ultraupdates.com

Many spiritual disciplines recommend retreats that often include a focus on prayer and fasting and re-aligning of our values with spiritual ones. Among Muslims, an entire month is devoted to this, and it is called Ramadan. Although the dates change, it is always in the early spring (April-May) and begins with a crescent moon and ends with a crescent moon. Fasting during daylight hours is an integral part of this ritual.

Some of the values that Muslims are encouraged to pray about include the need for forgiveness and for giving back to one's community. Even if we aren't Muslim, we can appreciate and borrow from this cultural reminder to pray more often, to find forgiveness in our hearts. We can feel encouraged in our journey by this reminder that giving back to one's community is a path that matters. That is the path of a caregiver.

*Inside the beautiful tapestry of a multicultural world, we are enriched by many reminders of ways to nourish the good seeds within us.*

## *April 30*

***"Nothing is softer or more flexible than water, yet nothing can resist it."***

—Lao Tzu

Water has that quality of being fluid, eminently shapeable and yet never losing its elemental sense and identity. The humility of water is a quality worth admiring and even emulating. We are often asked to shape ourselves or our days to the needs of our loved one. It's inevitable. And it can be humbling, especially since there are many messages in the world around us that would tell us to do otherwise.

My life as a primary caregiver often demanded a flexibility that is not required of me in other times of my life. Plans were often cancelled last minute, emergency needs took priority over other demands. There was a stronger-than-usual need to prioritize. As we adapt to our loved one's changing needs and fit our lives inside and around the shape of those needs, we can honor and bless this quality of humility. And yet honor our essence. We are still, elementally, the best of who we are.

*I can trust my own sense of self, even as I adapt and shape myself to the needs of this particular time and role.*

# May

## *May 1*

***"When I find myself in times of trouble, mother Mary comes to me, speaking words of wisdom, let it be. And in my hour of darkness she is standing right in front of me, speaking words of wisdom, let it be."***

—Paul McCartney

Whether or not our religious affiliation honors mother Mary, she is an icon of feminine and spiritual openheartedness. She is, to many of us, the ultimate mother—always extending her hand to help, always accepting us just as we are, always inviting our best selves forward. She is honored in many cultures and has been across centuries of time. The Beatles created this song that calls upon her to help all of us in our time of need, in our time of darkness.

These beautiful words and their equally beautiful melody invite us to imagine Mary shedding light on our own problems. Reminding us to let them be, reminding us to turn our troubles over to her open and accepting hands. We are not meant to "fix" everything.

*No matter what my belief system is, I can listen to this song and remember to let things be. I can envision a benevolent, loving, and holy mother helping me to do so.*

## *May 2*

**"Gratitude . . . turns what we have into enough, and more. It turns denial into acceptance, chaos to order, confusion to clarity. It can turn a meal into a feast, a house into a home, a stranger into a friend."**

—Melody Beattie

Shortly after my mother was widowed, after 69 years of marriage, a friend of hers gave her a small, round, smooth, and engraved stone. The word Gratitude was engraved upon it. Even as my mother was mourning the loss of her lifetime partner, seeing that stone on her table, picking it up and holding its solid smoothness in her hands, helped her to be reminded of all she had to be grateful for. The memories of a beautiful lifelong sense of teamwork, its gifts of children and grandchildren, her cozy apartment, her loved ones who visited often.

We all need reminders of what we have to be grateful for, but perhaps especially those who are experiencing much loss. A small stone that is a reminder of gratitude or a simple wall hanging with words that contain such a reminder are helpful to have around a loved one who needs special care. Gratitude is a quality the caregiver can also express and deepen. A cup of tea that is deeply appreciated all around can turn that meal into a feast and enhance the sense of being at home, no matter what new challenges are around the corner or in the air.

*Today I will be grateful for this time with my loved one and will encourage a sense of gratitude in both of us for the simple gifts of the day.*

## *May 3*

***"I have learned that when I am upset about what I see my mother going through and it knocks at my door in the dark hours, that if I put my warm hand over my heart and over my stomach, it helps calm me down."***

—Patricia Hoolihan, *journal*

The truth is that there were days when I was caring for my mom or my dad when I felt both raw and exhausted at the end of the day. During that time, I made a discovery: if the wings of fear or anxiety were batting away at my ability to sleep, I could calm them by placing one of my warm hands on my chest and the other on my stomach. I carry fear in both places. I sometimes felt fear for my mother, for my ability to hang in there and do a good job, for our family to get through this in a healthy and loving way.

Healing can happen in many ways, and this is a simple gesture which always helped calm me down and soothe me back into sleep, which I sorely needed. Intense caregiving creates a daily need for healing. It is helpful to be open to the many ways this can be found in the world around us.

*Today I will look for healing for my own tired and scared soul. There are many ways, and the warmth of my own healing hands is one of them.*

## *May 4*

***". . . [Caregivers] are an invisible workforce doing this work that we're born to do, to take care of each other. And yet it's not really valued in our culture."***

—Shoshana Berger, author, interview in
*Minneapolis Star Tribune*, Nov. 24, 2019

One of the difficulties for caregivers is this issue of how our culture doesn't seem, yet, to really value what we do. Thus, there are probably people in your world and perhaps even in your family who don't value what you contribute as a caregiver. Hopefully, this is changing as more light is being shed upon it. But it seems important to understand that most of us caregivers are paddling upstream in this regard—it's a hard paddle anyway, but the lack of understanding is yet another current one needs to work against.

It is not unheard of for a caregiver's efforts to be seen as "unnecessary" or "too much," so it is important to seek out support from people who do understand the value, the deep value of doing what we were "born to do": care for each other. I learned who to count on during those times and who to not count on. Such support is not yet built into the fabric of our culture but can be found among understanding persons.

*Our culture has a ways to go to honor the importance of being a caregiver and its human worth, so I need to seek support carefully. It helps to remember that caring for each other, among those who understand this, is what we were born to do.*

## *May 5*

***"A good laugh and a good long sleep are the two best cures in the doctor's book."***

—An Irish proverb

Overtired? Irritated? Overwhelmed? Worn out? Yes, it happens to all of us. You are not alone. There is no long-term solution; for most of us, the caregiving does not end until death brings a new challenge: the challenge of a final kind of loss and grief. So, meanwhile, how do we deal with the build-up of hard emotions?

Laughter. Hard to force, but often there is something about the absurdity of a day in this world that can be seen and shared in a humorous light. Look for it. And if that isn't available, rearrange your life to get a good night of sleep. Both are simple ways to take a break, to reenergize. It's important in the endurance run of caregiving to find easy and accessible ways to re-boot the system of your life and your caregiving. On a long run or marathon ski, people ingest energy drinks and calories. Think of sleep and laughter as ways to boost your energy for the next section of the trail.

*Humor and sleep are easy remedies that I can reach for when I feel worn down. Both are accessible and able to re-spark the energy that lives inside of me.*

# *May 6*

**"[Caregiving] constantly makes you wonder if you did enough."**

—Caroline Johnson

There seems to be an almost universal catch-22 to the art of caregiving. As a caregiver, you are giving more time and energy to your loved one than anyone else—even other family members. And because you are so close to the situation, you can see the many, many needs of this person who has been dear to you in one way or another. One of the emotional challenges and drains of the job is to wrestle with the limits of what is enough. Or rather, what can I realistically give and do any given day. The situation is often fluid and unpredictable. It is often not a limit that can be set in stone.

Garner support however you can. Create a mantra for yourself. Have a few people you can check in with when you need to draw a line, when you need to take a break, when you have other things you have to tend do. It is okay, and all will survive. Know that wondering if you are doing enough is a very common aspect of caregiving, and yet, it is most helpful to find ways to not let this kind of wondering get you down. Honor what you are doing. Take a break. Know you will be back, tomorrow or in a few days, a better person and caregiver.

*Even though I may wonder if I am doing enough,*
*I want to honor all that I am doing and*
*to know that, truly, is enough.*

## *May 7*

***"After nourishment, shelter and companionship, stories are the thing we need most in the world."***

—Philip Pullman

Stories! From the past or from the day. The exchange of stories, feeds all of our souls. Perhaps you or your loved one has a story to tell. My father was so very interested in my son's athleticism—my son was a cross-country ski racer at the time my father was slowing way down. My father loved the stories of the race, the close calls, how my son did. Sometimes I watched my mom's eyes light up over a story about one of my children or one of her many grandchildren.

Sometimes they had stories to tell of special events in their assisted living place or the story of a special visitor who had come the day before. Sometimes we spun off into familiar family stories we had known and retold for years. The exchange of stories is a vital way to connect. If I sense my loved one has a story to tell, then asking questions and listening are important ways to help draw out the story. I can also be generous as a storyteller—and intuitively honor the story at hand.

*On my road as a caregiver, it is important to honor the exchange of stories between me and my loved one. Listening is key here, but equally important is sharing our stories as well.*

## *May 8*

***"People respond to kindness even when medicine is ineffective, and in turn cultivating a kind heart is a cause of our own good health."***

—The Dalai Lama

Kindness can seem like an intangible quality, and yet we all recognize it when we see it in someone else and certainly when we are at the receiving end of it. Sometimes kindness means doing the things that need to get done but doing them in a cheerful and considerate way. Some of the tasks of caregivers are not very glamorous or fun, and it can be especially challenging to do those in the right spirit. And, yet, it will ultimately feel best even to ourselves if we make a bed, do the laundry, help someone move from one place to another, get something they need, and do it in a spirit of kindness rather than duty.

Yes, people do respond to kindness. Your loved one feels it when you are being kind. You will be able to tell because it will feel better to you as well. In looking back, I can think of days I wish I had pushed myself in some way past the worry, the rush, and sometimes the resentment and had given myself more wholly to kindness and love. Those days with my mother truly were fleeting. And the opportunity to dig deeper and deeper into my own ability to be kind and loving was right there every day.

*I will take care of my own good health today by being kind to myself as I am kind to my loved one. Kindness matters and makes the world a gentler place.*

## *May 9*

***"A mother is the one who fills your heart in the first place."***

—Amy Tan

Whether this meditation lands right on Mother's Day or near it, Mother's Day is a chance to do something special for or with our loved one. If we are caregiving for a mother, then the connection is direct. Time spent with her, a phone call, flowers, or a gift and card sent if you are not able to be there: all are ways to thank a mother and gratefully appreciate that she is here to celebrate the day with you.

If you are caregiving for someone other than your mother, you can use the day to honor motherhood in a myriad of ways. Perhaps it's a chance to share memories, have a conversation about their mother or yours, or honor any special mother you both have known. Recently, a relative of mine died, and in the days before his death, my cousin heard him calling out to his mother. The connection to a mother is powerful throughout an entire lifetime and beyond. Mother's Day gives us time to reflect on that.

*Mother's Day gives us all a chance to honor motherhood in a way that celebrates the gifts received and to honor the mother/love inside our hearts.*

## *May 10*

**"If I could save time in a bottle . . . "**

—Lyric by Jim Croce

This hit song from 1974 was written by a father to his infant child. If he could save time in a bottle, he would do so to spend it with his child, to go through life and time with that child. Sadly, Croce was killed in a plane crash, and so his life was cut short. But the desire to spend time with a loved one, the iconic words, and catchy melody do live on in time.

Time is an element that philosophers and writers and scientists have wrestled with for millennia. And time is something we share with a loved one. Perhaps limited time. Time on this journey can feel long and slow and bountiful; it can feel rushed and scarce. But perhaps time, with its many multifaceted angles, is the essence of what we share with our loved one, and with all who are a part of our daily journey.

*Today I can appreciate the simple gift of sharing time with the people I love.*

## *May 11*

***"But are we treating the elderly members of the family with an empathetic love and respect? Do they die surrounded with care?"***

—Karen Armstrong

Armstrong, a leading spiritual scholar and synthesizer, poses questions that she believes are key to assessing if we, as communities, are striving for spiritual meaning and development. The above question is important enough to be asked by her, and its answer is often in the hands of caregivers all over the world. The question is directed at individuals and families but also institutions and larger communities. For how we care for the elderly reveals our ability to show compassion and to honor hard-earned wisdom.

As a caregiver, your contribution may seem insignificant as a part of a larger whole. Certainly, some days it feels that way. But caregivers need and deserve to be honored for the way all of us are stepping in to answer the question posed by Armstrong. Every elderly or physically or mentally challenged person who is cared for with love and respect contributes to a greater sense of connection and wholeness and makes the world a better place. The ripple effect is immeasurable, but surely nurtures a wider and deepening sense of community.

*For today I can know that I am doing my part to make the world a better place by surrounding my loved one with care in a loving and respectful way.*

## *May 12*

***"I began to see that hope, however feeble its foundation, bespeaks allegiance to every unlikely beauty on this earth."***

—David James Duncan

There are days when hope runs thin—hope for less pain in our loved one, hope for a different outcome than we are witnessing, hope for the ability to keep our own inner fires burning. The impact of a long and arduous road is that there are moments when one feels like hope is beyond reach. And yet, the beauty of the natural world is always there within reach in a multitude of ways, and its beauty shines a light that falls equally on all.

A stunning sunrise, the aroma and deep color of even one rose, a brilliantly yellow bird singing and fluttering nearby, the deer that appears at the edge of the yard. Sunlight on a brick wall in the early morning, the slant of afternoon light falling upon a loved one's face, the half moon lighting up the landscape of night. All of these moments of natural beauty, and many, many more are awaiting our attention. The enduring and yet ephemeral qualities of beauty in the natural world carry a spirit thread of hope, a reminder that we all share something both eternal and fleeting and worthy of being cherished.

*On days when my hope and energy run low,
I can always look to the natural world to revive,
comfort, and remind me of a deep and ongoing
beautiful energy, there to inspire me.*

## *May 13*

***"Love is that condition in which the happiness of another person is essential to your own."***

—Robert Heinlein

Those we are taking care of are in the process of losing strengths and abilities they have, in most cases, known and enjoyed for years. It is often a time of waning confidence, of unsure footing as each day seems to bring new challenges. A touchstone for any caregiver is the ability to have empathy for this process and a sense of merciful understanding for ourselves and for how difficult it is to watch this.

Yes, to know that one is still lovable is a core human need. Even a whisper of love—a smile as one enters the room, a gentle voice over the telephone, a loving note in the mailbox—helps restore a sense of dignity. Although much is being lost, it is essential to also honor what is still here: a beloved person. At their core, they need to be reminded that, in spite of all the changes, they are still loved and cherished.

*Today I will honor my own efforts as a whisper of love, one that sends out a ripple effect that matters.*

## *May 14*

***"God, grant me the serenity to accept the things I cannot change."***

—First line of "The Serenity Prayer"

When someone is in need of care, their physical, mental, or emotional capacities have diminished or altered in some ways. There's a lot of commonality here across a broad range of situations but also unique challenges for each person. Time spent wishing things are different than they really are most often works against us.

As difficult as some realizations are to come to, there is a palpable sense of relief that accompanies acceptance of what is beyond our control. And often, on this road, much is beyond our control: everything from the imperfect places most of our loved ones live inside of, to mistakes made, to disappointments among family helpers. Accepting what can't be changed frees up our energy to work with what we can change—and often, initially, that means our attitude and our expectations.

*Today I will take a moment to honor and accept the current aspect of this journey that I cannot change and will find more serenity by adjusting my attitude and expectations.*

## *May 15*

***" . . . a warm, unafraid glance or gentle touch can say much more than words."***

—Kirsten DeLeo

For years, I have taught a writing class at the assisted living facility where my mother spent the last four years of her life. Sometimes I have them write about what delights them or lifts their spirits. Inevitably it is a phone call or a visit from the special people in their lives. It is the grandchild's warm voice over the phone. It is the surprise visit from a son or daughter or an old friend. It is the nurse aide who comes in with a friendly smile on her face.

While we might at times be wondering how to say what needs saying, how to bring up the difficult conversation whose time has come, so much of what matters is our emotional presence around the words. A gentle touch or an empathetic look exchanged with a loved one provides an essential framework that helps to carry the necessary words. That connection eye to eye, soul to soul, conveys the most important message of all—that your loved one matters. It requires an open heart and courage.

*A loving and gentle and full-hearted presence carries a message stronger than any words; it is a message of love and respect, of being here, in a full-hearted way, for you.*

## *May 16*

***"We cannot live for ourselves alone. Our lives are connected by a thousand invisible threads and along these sympathetic fibers, our actions run as causes and return to us as results."***

—Herman Melville

This is such a beautiful image about the interconnectedness of life. I love the visual of a thousand invisible threads; I imagine multiple colors, woven in unimaginable and unseen ways. It is so easy to fall into thinking our actions don't matter or don't amount to much. Yet, when I think back to all the times I crossed the threshold into my mother's assisted living, I am grateful for those threads of love. I hope I cherished them as fully as I think I would today.

This is also a beautiful way to imagine the exchange between us and our loved ones. It honors the golden rule in a visual way; how would I want to be greeted or treated if I were the vulnerable one? Most of us will at some point get our turn.

*I join the better part of humanity as I find ways to live not only for myself but for my loved ones as well. The energy exchange between us deepens and enriches me every day.*

## *May 17*

***"Without loving kindness for ourselves it is difficult, if not impossible, to genuinely feel it for others."***

—Pema Chodron

Truly, there is no other path that challenges us to balance self-love with love of another than caregiving—except for the path of parenthood. And so, the path of caregiving is a great opportunity. As parents of young and growing children, we are building confidence in an unseen but beautifully potential future. In caregiving, we are much more focused on the here and now and on making what is left of the journey as meaningful as possible. There is a different mindset.

Yet what the two paths have in common are the huge amount of responsibility and the ongoing need to both care for ourselves and for our loved ones who need us. The best parents are often those with a strong sense of self, a solid core. And so, too, a healthy caregiver feeds his or her inner core. Doing this requires a commitment to be loving toward ourselves, even when we are filled with doubt and fatigue. We all have ways to feed our inner core; granting ourselves permission, in a spirit of loving kindness, will deepen our ability to genuinely care for others.

*Am I being as kind to myself as I want to be for others? This is a question that invites us into deeper layers of love and acceptance.*

## *May 18*

***"I needed to focus on the reality of the disease and not any feelings of rejection or futility I was experiencing when my best laid plans went awry."***

—Kris Berggren

My friend received a phone call in the middle of the day that her mother had escaped from the memory care unit and was found wandering a block away. Her mother was skillful enough to follow visitors out the locked door and look like she knew what she was doing. This, just when my friend thought her mother was settling in to her new place of residence.

These are the emergency moments where one might initially feel very frustrated and/or disappointed. One more plan that would have to be renegotiated in some way. Learning to not take this personally was enormously helpful—although easier said than done. Her mother was in the grips of the disease of memory loss. An understanding of the disease helps foster compassion for those in its grip. Adapting to the ever-changing and very real expressions of any disease is a big part of a caregiver's role.

*Understanding the disease my loved one struggles with is key to not taking his or her actions personally. This frees me to focus more clearly on the needs at hand.*

## *May 19*

**"It is only with the heart that one can see rightly; what is essential is invisible to the eye."**

*—The Little Prince*

My friend whose mother spent her last months in a memory care unit told me a story one day. Near the end, a family member recorded someone saying the "Lord's Prayer" in Norwegian, the language her mother had spoken as a child and left behind a long time ago. Despite a seriously impaired memory, tears shone in her eyes as she listened to this prayer she had known all of her life in the language of her childhood. All who were in the room felt the depth of those tears.

This moment went right to the heart of who she was and became a treasured memory for them all after she passed on. This story sheds light on how matters of the heart are truly more important than anything else, especially when someone's days are limited or numbered. The details we manage on a daily basis can overwhelm us, but finding time to honor heartfelt sharing will always remain in our hearts and memories as our most important contribution.

*What is on my loved one's heart these days?*
*Tuning in, we can find a way to enter and*
*celebrate elemental heart-needs.*

## *May 20*

***"Walking, much like singing, steadies the mind."***

—Stephen Levine

There are many experiences along this journey that can set off anxiety and worry. Any medical concerns sound alarm bells, and then there are all the schedule questions and tidal waves of emotion. So one needs multiple ways to soothe anxiety and to quiet a tendency to worry. There are many ways, but two simple ones are walking or singing.

Walking, if one is able, is a beautiful panacea. Moving one's body in a rhythmic way helps clear the cobwebs of questions from the mind, helps ease a tightness in the chest, helps calm every nerve in your body. All the better if you can walk outside where the fresh air and quiet gifts of nature surround you. Singing, even a quiet hum to oneself, is also a great way to calm an anxious moment.

*If my mind feels uneasy or overwhelmed, I can take myself for a walk or remember to sing to myself. These simple tools can help me move through today in a calmer way.*

## *May 21*

***"Sometimes I go about with pity for myself and all the while Great Winds are carrying me across the sky."***

—Ojibwe saying

When the going gets rough, when the path feels lonely or dogged, we can always remember to turn to the natural world for solace, comfort, encouragement. Winds, like opening wings of spirit, can calm or energize a day that is in need of a wider perspective. The night my father died, it was a sky full of stars that wrapped its embrace around me. Twinkles of light and the depth of the deeply dark sky seemed to understand what I had just experienced. Likewise, a walk near water, trees, green leaves, or blossoms of any kind can lift a tired heart as it opens in need.

We can be grateful to a variety of cultural traditions in this world for reminding us of ways to remember how the earth cares for us, how we are ultimately part of a universal web of life. When worn down by the difficulties and ongoing-ness of caregiving, this Ojibwe saying reminds us to listen to the wind, the healing power of the natural world, and let it carry us through the day's needs.

*Today I will seek the power and solace of the Great Winds and the healing power of all that it carries.*

## *May 22*

***"We shall never know all the good that a simple smile can do."***

—Mother Teresa

Sometimes as caregivers, we can get caught up in all the details. The schedules, the aides, the medications, the doctor appointments. But more than once, what I witnessed in my mother's last months is that the smile on the face of a helper who entered her room made all the difference between a hard moment and one filled with sunlight.

A genuine caring smile on my face as I entered her room—or on the faces of other visiting family members or on the faces of staff members at her facility—always visibly warmed her heart. It is not easy to be the one in need, and when she felt like people wanted to be there for her, this helped ease her mind. The simple gift of a warm sincere smile can be a beacon of light shining into the darkness of loneliness and of the loss that comes with limited abilities.

*My smile can be the simple gift of today—*
*for my loved one and for myself.*

## *May 23*

***"It was interesting to see how our roles had reversed; Mom now needed me to give her the care she had given me as a child."***

—Geraldine Ferraro

The role reversal that is a part of caregiving comes as a surprise to almost everyone. We get used to it, but there is something rather mind-boggling about it at the same time. Here is someone who took care of us over the years, perhaps imperfectly, but did so. Here is someone who used to be so capable in so many ways and now needs help in elemental ways. The changes, even if they happen rather slowly, can be difficult to fully comprehend.

No one of us really expects to grow old or become ill in any way. Sure, we know everyone grows old and many do become ill, but the actual experience almost always comes as a surprise and requires huge emotional adjustments. If we are lucky, we are giving back to someone who gave much to us over the years. Even more challenging is caregiving for someone with whom we have had a more distant or tangled relationship. Embedded in a role reversal is an opportunity to say thank you from the past, to take our turn where it is needed.

*Today I will honor the role I have taken on and appreciate its reversal. I can be grateful for the times when I needed and received similar care, as I pass on this kind of care.*

## *May 24*

***"Somewhere the child I was is wailing***
***I grieve the loss of mother***
***Accept that for now I am mothering her***
***And myself as well."***

—Judith E. Prest

Whether we are tending to a parent or another loved one, an integral part of our caregiving involves a heightened awareness of who this person has been to us and for us. That gift lives inside of our hearts, and the awareness can flood us with gratefulness for what we once had with this loved one. At the same time, the fraying edges of its changes and loss can humble us, make us raw with grief at certain and often unpredictable moments, and live somewhere inside of us at all times.

It is a fascinating dual thread that as we "mother" or nurture and care for this person, we are also caring for ourselves. Grief needs kindness and gentle time. Often, so does your loved one. As you reach out, nurturing in the way you best know how to, you are also nurturing yourself. The quiet wailing inside of us, heard perhaps only occasionally or subtly, also deserves our attention and care. Grief and gratitude are woven within the tapestry of love.

*As a caring person, I can find ways to nurture*
*my loved one and to gently nurture*
*the grieving parts of me as well.*

## *May 25*

***"To love means never to be afraid of the windstorms of life. Should you shield the canyons from the windstorms, you would never see the true beauty of their carvings."***

—Elisabeth Kubler-Ross

This is a beautiful image for how love marks us. Scars, woundedness, and exhaustion are ways that the windstorms of caregiving impact the rock of our love, of our very being. Carvings! And if you have ever stood near a canyon or mountain or rockface of any size, then you have probably been riveted by the designs and textures carved across its surface.

As you face the windstorms of caregiving, you will sometimes find them to be gentle breezes out of the west or relentless gusts from the north. Winds can stir up everything that has been rooted and tear leaves and branches off trees. And yet a morning breeze out of the east can fill one with fresh air and hopes. All of these winds shape us as subtly and invisibly as they carve rockfaces all over our planet.

*As I lovingly face the many moods of the windstorms of caregiving, my soul is being shaped and carved in beautiful ways that often only slowly become visible.*

## *May 26*

***"Everything is a gift. The degree to which we are awake to this truth is a measure of our gratefulness and gratefulness is a measure of our aliveness."***

—Brother David Stendal-Rast

That 5:00 am phone call? Hard to feel grateful for that. The to-do list that never quite gets crossed off? Hard to not feel consumed by that. However, what we can feel grateful for is our own ability to respond to the crisis call. We can, over and over again, feel grateful for what we have been able to do in any one day and let go of what we didn't get to. Our own health, our availability to give care to our loved one, these are treasured moments in a long lifetime.

Being grateful, as this spiritual leader of our times reminds us, is connected to a feeling of being deeply alive. Many people these days are keeping gratitude journals; this is a very helpful way to remind ourselves of all the gifts in our lives. Gifts of shared time, gifts of each day, gifts of having loved ones whom we feel connected to—all are worth taking time, even just a few moments, to appreciate.

*Even if I am having a busy day, I can find a few moments to appreciate, even to write down, what I am grateful for today.*

## *May 27*

***"Nature is the one song of praise that never stops singing."***

—Richard Rohr

The double duty of caring for ourselves and for another loved one on a regular basis often leaves us with the feeling that there are not enough hours in a day. That tight squeeze, that sense of overwhelm is a very human response. Yet there is another way to look at it: a full life is a gift to be embraced and celebrated. There's a vibrancy to living and loving fully.

What helps us shift from overwhelm to appreciation of the fullness of our lives? Often it's a change of attitude for which we can reach. Yet nature is also a tangible reminder for how to move ourselves in the direction of praise for life. Nature is all around us, reminding us how to celebrate abundance, praising the gift of life through all of its seasons and moods.

*When I need to hear a song of praise, I can look and listen to the natural around me—somewhere, in some way, it will sing to me.*

## *May 28*

**"When fun gets deep enough, it can heal the world."**

—the Oaqui

An often overlooked and helpful element for caregiving is to have fun. This can be easily lost among the serious concerns of daily details for someone who is losing strength in any way. Fun often centers around something to celebrate—perhaps a birthday, a special day, an achievement by someone in the family, a special event of any sort.

Fun often centers around doing something corny or doing the ordinary in a slightly out of the ordinary way. Puzzle day with corny hats on or cribbage with a special drink treat. A new decoration for the apartment wall. Fun and easily lighthearted moments and activities bring a special light to the world of caregiving. It's an important light.

*No matter what the struggles are for my loved one or for myself, we can find ways to make our time together fun.*

## *May 29*

***"The fragrance from the oils of the lavender plant is believed to help promote calmness and wellness. It's also said to help reduce stress, anxiety, and possibly even mild pain."***

—Healthline.com

When my mother was in the hospital and then in the care of hospice, one of the tools we all received were small vials containing the scent of lavender. When I uncapped it and waved it under my mother's nose, she would breathe it in and smile. We took turns because breathing in that beautiful scent always helped me as well. An aroma that invites a wave of relaxation, it carries a calming quality on the wings of breath.

Lavender has been used as far back in time as ancient Egypt for healing purposes. Easily available in most stores, it is inexpensive. It is also known to help people who have sleep issues. When I open the lavender I now always carry in my purse, I am flooded with nostalgia for the sweet moments of relief this simple gift brought to both my mother and me and other family members during difficult moments.

*I am grateful for the simple tools, like the scent of lavender, which can calm and brighten my days as a caregiver. Lavender is a gift from the earth itself.*

## *May 30*

***"It is hard to listen to others when the pains and troubles of our own lives are clamoring for attention. But if we listen to our needs and wants, that listening can free us to learn to become truly present to the inner deep and fragile beauty of those under our care."***

—Henri Nouwen

The path of caregiving is such a dual-sided experience. Caring for another inevitably requires us to care for ourselves. The two are interchangeable, although the struggle to achieve balance is daily and always in flux. There are so many factors at work. The largest toll exacted upon many caregivers is the way one's own needs seem to always be put on the back burner. After a while they accumulate, and this accumulation begins to weigh us down.

To heal such an accumulation demands our attention: writing about one's needs, talking about them, finding even simple ways to care for ourselves is essential. Listening to ourselves is the opening to being able to really appreciate, as Nouwen so beautifully states, the "deep and fragile beauty" of our loved ones.

*When I feel emotionally removed from my caregiving, it is time to be kind to myself, to care for myself. This is how I find my way back to the intricate beauty of my relationship with my loved one.*

## *May 31*

***"The willingness of America's veterans to sacrifice for our country has earned them our lasting gratitude."***

—Jeff Miller

Memorial Day, always held on the last Monday of May, began in the aftermath of the Civil War. It is a day set aside to honor those who have given their lives for a larger cause—for our country. The purpose of Memorial Day is to remember, honor, and appreciate the fallen. Their sacrifices truly made and continue to make a collective difference. My father and uncles served in WWII, and all miraculously returned home safely. My mother and other family members also made great sacrifices at that time.

One Memorial Day, I helped my Mom, in her later years, into her wheelchair, and we rolled over to the cemetery behind the church near her assisted living facility. The setting itself was simple and tender. Our quiet conversation was drenched with gratitude and a sober awareness of life's fragility. Even though it wasn't our hometown cemetery and it wasn't a military cemetery, it was a place and a way to honor the spirit of the day. It was a day to honor the memory of her husband, my father, and our other loved ones.

*Let me take a few moments with my loved one over Memorial Day weekend to honor our collective memories of those we have lost and mourn.*

# June

## *June 1*

***"Most of all, differences of opinion are opportunities for learning."***

—Terry Tempest Williams

One of the difficulties inherent in caregiving is differences of opinion, whether with others on our team of caregivers or even sometimes with our loved one. Family dynamics are often a challenging part of this journey, for crises tend to bring out the divisions and wide array of coping mechanisms already present. There were moments when I felt that the underlying family tensions made a difficult job only harder. But it is part of the process, not something separate from it.

Truly, such moments are opportunities for more communication. Of course, people are going to respond differently to situations as they arise. I can see this so much more clearly in retrospect. There is more of a demand for negotiating these differences when caregiving is in a state of crisis or change. For most families, this is difficult terrain—made more passable by listening to each other and respecting each other's way of coping.

*When I am struggling with a difference of opinion, I hope to approach it as an opportunity for learning and understanding more—about myself, about my fellow caregivers, about our loved one.*

## *June 2*

**"Every now and again take a good look at something not made with hands—a mountain, a star, the turn of a stream. There will come to you wisdom and patience and solace and, above all, the assurance that you are not alone in the world."**

—Sidney Lovett

Loneliness is a feeling that comes over most people, at least from time to time, and which everyone wrestles with in their own way. I have heard caregivers speak of feeling lonely; they may feel more tied down compared to other friends, and it can feel like one's world is shrinking. Pangs of loneliness can enter a day and demand attention.

Talking to a trusted friend always helps one feel less lonely. But there are other ways also. Whatever gifts of nature are around you—trees, stars, a stream, or lake—can also bring you solace. Take a good look, as Lovett says, and let the qualities of steadfastness enter you. Listen to the trees—they speak of a deep and timeless way of being. The wisdom of the natural world invites all of us in and embraces us.

*When feeling lonely or in need of solace, I can turn to the natural world around me. In so many ways and through so many forms, its wisdom will help hold me up and keep me in good company.*

## *June 3*

***"Be patient with everyone but above all with yourself."***

—Francis de Sales

The road to recovery from difficult health issues or the road to acceptance of a life-long and life-draining situation are roads that require deep pockets of patience. There are steps forward, then backward, then forward again. It is often the many small steps—emphasis on the word small—that add up to anything. Hurried impatience is not a friend on these roads, although we will often recognize its presence.

Suffice it to say that the role of caregiver gives one ample opportunity to practice patience. These wise words from a holy person of the 1600s remind us of the challenges humans have faced across time. As caregivers, we often need to exercise patience with our loved ones and with the imperfections of the systems we are dealing with—medically, with families, and with any care facility. But above all, we can appreciate the reminder to be patient with ourselves.

*Patience will help me take the wisest next step and will help me to know when acceptance rather than action is most needed.*

*June 4*

***"We have thousands of opportunities every day to be grateful: for having good weather, to have slept well last night, to be able to get up, to be healthy, to have enough to eat. . . . There's opportunity upon opportunity to be grateful; that's what life is."***

—Brother David Stendal-Rast

I love the simplicity and meaningful message of this entire quote, but in particular of that last line. I find it especially true if you change the juxtaposition: that's what life is, the opportunity upon opportunity to be grateful. Although the stress and demands of caregiving may crowd out gratefulness, we can always make room for it. The opportunity is always there. And gratitude is a deep way to find energy in this world and on our life path.

There is a lot to be grateful for as a human being and as a caregiver. Food and shelter and breath—yes. Also, as a caregiver, we are invited to enter into a deep way of loving, often at a sacred and most vulnerable time in our loved one's life. There is a richness here, a deeply embedded sense of meaning. This relationship matters, our presence matters; it is so nourishing to pause and be grateful for this richness.

*Especially if I am feeling stressed, I need to carve out time to remember all that I am grateful for today, in this moment. This awareness deeply energizes me.*

## *June 5*

***"In our life there is a single color, as on an artist's palette, which provides the meaning of life and art. It is the color of love."***

—Marc Chagall

Color in Chagall's artwork is both brilliantly beautiful and beautifully brilliant. He is most known for his paintings and stained glass work. Color was his medium, but in his own words the color that provided the true meaning for his art and his life is the color of love. The color of love is an interesting concept, one worth pondering and borrowing. How might color brighten up our days as a caregiver?

There are many ways for color to be an expression of love—the beauty of flowers is an obvious one. This is why flowers are such a popular gift for important occasions. Yet there are many other ways that color can be an expression of love. Perhaps a new sweater or blanket for your loved one, in their favorite shade of blue. Or a new scarf or tablecloth can be a way that color can uplift one's heart. More than once, my mother let me know that the color I was wearing was something she appreciated. We can express ourselves through color, but above all, we can express our love through color.

*I can look around me and find creative ways to let the color of love enter my world and day.*

## *June 6*

***"Love that stammers, that stutters, is apt to be the love that loves best."***

—Gabriela Mistral

This is a great reminder that we all make mistakes, we all fall short of our own ideas of perfection, and yet, our intention to love is what really matters. There were times when I made mistakes as a caregiver: I didn't ask enough questions; I should have called in my cousin who is a priest; I should have stayed longer on one particular day when my mother later injured herself. Some days, I definitely missed cues that I might not have missed if I had been more tuned in to my intuition and less exhausted. Other days, it was easier to feel I had done the right thing.

I could have used regular reminders that I didn't need to be perfect. There was a sharp learning curve going on; suddenly I needed to be part nurse, part consumer advocate, part health advocate, and always sensitive to how and when to share information. I/we made mistakes. But what I want to honor through it all, through the mistakes and stammers, is the power of the language of love.

*Caregivers are conveyors of love, even on days when the love on our tongue stutters or stammers. Let us honor the deep language of love we are living.*

## *June 7*

**"When we talk of tomorrow, the gods laugh."**

—Chinese proverb

One of the beautiful and wise slogans of the 12-step program is "A day at a time." Some days, this is harder to remember than others. But it is a good one to keep returning to when our wandering minds want to worry about the future. How many times have all of us worried about something in the future and then the problem took care of itself in some unexpected way.

In the world of caregiving, there are many forces at work. Although we may often feel like time stands still, in other ways, time can be like an iron that presses out the wrinkles of worry. Each day's answer becomes clear as it is needed. And often unforeseen moments help make this happen.

*Living a day at a time as a caregiver allows me peace of mind and makes way for the universe to both surprise and help me.*

## *June 8*

***"Oh Great Spirit . . . Sweeten my heart and fill me with light."***

—Paul War Cloud

In lessons on learning to draw, there is a focus on how light bounces off of the textures of objects which are being drawn. Light disperses differently whether it is reflecting off of a smooth or rough surface. Artists focus on capturing the nuances of light in a way that I find instructive. How does our view of the world around us or the day in front of us connect to the light in our hearts? How do the objects or challenges in front of us disperse light; where are the highlights and where are the shadows?

On days when the shadows loom, we can reach out to a Great Spirit and asked to be filled with light. We can always ask; this quote models how powerful and direct such a request can be. Light is a gift of perspective, and when light enters our heart, everything it reflects upon and from will have a sweeter feel and a more comforting texture.

*If our day feels dark with shadows, we can ask whatever Great Spirit we believe in to let light enter our hearts and our day. Such a light will reflect and illumine what I see and feel.*

## *June 9*

***"Yesterday is history, tomorrow is a mystery, today is a gift of God, which is why we call it the present."***

—Bill Keane

We human beings are so easily distracted that we need to be continually reminded to come back into the present. Meditation practices of all kinds focus on this. Certainly, as caregivers, we have many distractions in our lives. We often have multiple roles other than that of caregiver. And within caregiving, there is often a wide range of responsibilities.

When I think of this, I envision a juggler balancing many balls. Yet the truth of a successful juggler is that their concentration is deep inside the present moment. The moment a juggler worries about catching that next ball, they often fumble. Of course, this takes enormous amounts of practice, and yet, so does the ability to live inside the present moment.

*Today's gift is right here in the present moment;*
*however I might describe it,*
*let me breathe it in fully.*

## *June 10*

***"If I am not good to myself, how can I expect anyone else to be good to me?"***

—Maya Angelou

Today's meditation is an official reminder to find and take the time to be good to ourselves. It's surprisingly easy to forget to do so. Often this gets pushed to the sidelines, the back burner, or we run out of room for it on our caregiving to-do list. We can't expect others to do it for us, and besides, we have the best sense of our own needs and ways to find comfort.

So, we need to make it a priority to be good to ourselves. To explore one or more of the many ways to do so. There are the restful or rejuvenating activities such as a walk in nature, exercise, time with friends, time alone, music in any form. So important also is how we talk to ourselves, how we honor and affirm who we are in the world.

*Today I will put being good to myself at the top of the list and let it lead me to a way of thinking or an activity that will revitalize me.*

## *June 11*

***"There is a time to keep silence and a time to speak."***

—Ecclesiastes 3

This beautiful passage tells us of the importance of discernment, which is a word for spiritual guidance. What and when to speak? What to keep to ourselves? A friend tells of caring for his father who suffered from memory loss. There was the time when the difficult conversation had to happen about why he needed to move into a memory care unit. But there were many other days when the stories he told did not need to be corrected or set inside the correct time frame. They only needed to be listened to and heard. He only needed to be heard.

It may be a time to be silent if our words will be harmful or hurtful in some way—or unnecessary. It may be a time to speak when important information needs to be shared and understood. Discernment relies on a quiet spiritual center; all of us human beings have this resource within us.

*Today I will listen for where I need to keep silent and where I need to speak up. There is a beautiful time for each.*

## *June 12*

***"This comes up all the time in mechanical work. A hang-up. You just sit and stare and think . . . and go away and come back again, and after a while the unseen factors start to emerge."***

—Robert M. Pirsig

There are many problems that arise when one is caregiving a loved one. The problems range from finances, to dealing with delicate emotional issues, to translating medical needs, to finding safe housing, to adapting to continually changing needs, and more. It is striking what an intellectually challenging endeavor it can be.

These quoted words from the author of *Zen and the Art of Motorcycle Maintenance* remind us that our minds and hearts are always at work. Many puzzles are solved by walking away from them and returning with a fresh eye. There is a kind of trust, a form of letting go and yet a keen awareness that can bring most problems into the focus of a solution. Time itself helps us to see the need and the solution in a most helpful way. Rather than force an answer, we can take a step back and trust a deeper process is at work.

*Today I remind myself that a solution is near at hand for today's problem. I can allow the answer to emerge.*

## *June 13*

***"You will find, as you look back upon your life, that the moments when you really lived are the moments when you have done things in the spirit of love."***

—Henry Drummond

Some of my favorite memories of my mother in her last years are the times we did special occasion baking. This was a ritual that she and I and other family members had done since I was a child. In my youth, the baking was intense and complicated: many kinds of cookies and breads. In her last years, we whittled it down to one or two simple recipes—more than that made her anxious.

This is a memory of love because giving away baked goods was a way she showed her love and care to family and friends all of her life. Baking and sharing food was a deeply-rooted gesture of love for her, and pleasant and easy time was spent helping her to carry it on. Almond bark melted around pretzels, almonds, and crunchy cereal will always remind me of those special afternoons shared with her and her delight as we placed them in small bags and tied them with colored ribbon so she could give to her neighbors, her new friends, to those people who helped her with her every day needs and to special visitors. She was happy to have a colorful and tasteful way to say thank you to the people in her life.

*Simple rituals can contain multiple generations worth of love. As I honor a simple ritual with my loved one, I am honoring many years' worth of loving gestures.*

## *June 14*

***"There's nowhere you can be that isn't where you're meant to be . . . "***

—John Lennon

There are some factors of caregiving that are uncomfortable, at least from time to time. Such feelings might include a sense of inadequacy for the task at hand or frustrations with myriad aspects of this role or the discouragement one encounters along the way. There were certainly days when I wondered if I was really cut out for it, if I was really the right person for the role. I often wondered if the job I was doing was good enough.

Over and over again, it helped to remember that I was right where I was meant to be. Even in my imperfections, I was still the right person for the moment, and furthermore, I was grateful for the opportunity. When we look around, we can see how right it is to be in this role, sharing it with other loved ones, sharing this special time with the one who is most vulnerable.

*This role is where I am meant to be right now in this life. I will honor it, imperfections and all.*

## *June 15*

***" . . . to appreciate beauty and find the best in others; to leave the world a bit better whether by a healthy child, a garden patch, a redeemed social condition; to know even one life has breathed easier because you have lived—this is to have succeeded."***

—Ralph Waldo Emerson

Emerson, a writer and philosopher and leader of the Transcendentalism movement of the 1800s, was a leading thinker of his day. Many of his wise words have lived forward in time. In this beautiful quote is embedded a cornerstone of caregiving. At its simplest, our efforts are intended to help our loved one breathe easier, to help our loved one through a vulnerable time of their life. So often overlooked by our culture, such efforts cannot really be quantified.

Yet this deep thinker from centuries ago gives us words of confirmation—a gift that travels through time. Helping even one person to breathe more easily can be considered a successful contribution to this world, perhaps even in a timeless way. No fireworks here, no huge accomplishment listed—just helping another to breathe more easily. We do so through many small but dependable gestures.

*When questioning my own sense of accomplishment, I can find confirmation in Emerson's definition of success; I am making an important contribution as a caregiver.*

## *June 16*

***"May you be content with yourself just the way you are. Let this knowledge settle into your bones, and allow your soul the freedom to sing, dance, praise and love. It is there for each and every one of us."***

—St. Teresa of Avila

These words come as a comfort to anyone, but perhaps especially to a stressed-out or worn-down caregiver. Just meeting ourselves right where we are can often be a relief. I found that caregiving often created doubt in myself in strange ways; was I doing enough, doing it the right way, how could I possibly keep it all going? Acknowledging the intensity of the role and of that time in my life was helpful. Letting the knowledge of that moment of time sink in, or in St. Teresa's words, settle into our bones, can help immensely.

Embracing the moment allows us to find the song and dance and praise and love in it all. As this holy woman reminds us, such an ability to embrace the here and now is accessible to all of us. It is possible to feel contentment in this time of caregiving. It's worth reaching for, even as it seems hard to find some days.

*Available to me at any time is the choice to accept who I am just as I am—to find contentment in how I am navigating my role as a caregiver. For today, that is more than enough.*

## *June 17*

***"Every day is a god, each day is a god, and holiness holds forth in time."***

—Annie Dillard

Truly, each day is a gift. Each breath of life, every morning that we are able to awaken and move into our day, every connection with a loved one. It is so easy to slide into taking things for granted—like a new day. What aids the taking for granted is feeling overwhelmed or moving speedily through what must be done.

It doesn't take much time to appreciate the gift of each day; it only takes an awareness of its preciousness. Those who have been near death or are nearing death know the gift of a day more acutely than others. Awareness of the possibility of the end brings the gift of each day into focus. As caregivers, we can zero into this focus, this deep well of gratefulness for a new day. Such awareness is guaranteed to make us better human beings and caregivers.

*Today I will take a deep breath and appreciate the many gifts all around me, embedded in this day.*

## *June 18*

***"Compassion is not a relationship between the healer and the wounded. It's a relationship between equals."***

—Pema Chodron

A friend of mine walked in to visit his ailing father during a time when he was feeling guilty about all the gifts in his life, for his cousin of the same age had just died. His father tuned in to my friend's struggle as well as the collective family pain. At one point, his father turned to him and said ever so gently, "You deserve your loving family and beautiful life that you have created—you deserve it all."

Those words entered him deeply and provided the healing he needed that day. The exchange between caregiver and loved one can be a rich one if we attune to all the ways in which we can both give and receive. We are all both wounded and capable of providing moments of healing to each other.

*Help me to remember that though my loved one is more vulnerable at this time, they have much to offer in often subtle and surprising ways.*

## *June 19*

***"Just watch this moment, without trying to change it at all. What is happening? What do you feel? What do you see? What do you hear?"***

—Jon Kabat-Zinn

Caregiving is an enormous undertaking with so many facets to it. It is emotionally laden with years of history. Often the changes going on are hard to keep up with and adapt to, and there is always some element of ongoing grief—both for loved one and for caregiver. Time can be hard to come by, but taking it when you can to observe all that is happening and all that you are going through is enormously helpful and even healing.

For some, reflection time in the morning or evening, at day's beginning or end, is a helpful time to look at one's life. Maybe your best reflection time is when you are alone in your car. There is power in watching and recognizing and honoring all that is happening. It is a way to honor the richness of the caregiving journey with all of its challenges and tender moments. Allow that richness to emerge as you pay attention to and open your heart to all that you are seeing and hearing and feeling.

*My heart is full as I blindly make my way along this caregiving path—I am grateful for that and feel it more powerfully when I take time to observe this fullness.*

## *June 20*

***"If there is any immortality to be had among us human beings, it is certainly only in the love that we leave behind. Fathers like mine don't ever die."***

—Leo Buscaglia

There are many words used for father: Dad, Daddy, Pops, Papa, Dada, and many more. If we are caring for our father, Father's Day is a great opportunity to let him know what he has been to us over the years. Through spoken or written word, we can articulate what we have learned and reminisce about important shared moments. If we are caregiving for a mother, spouse, or other family member, we can use the day to honor our loved one's father or our own.

Sometimes simply sharing a memory about one's father can deepen our appreciation for what Father's Day is meant to be about. Years after my father passed on, I find myself quoting him: his words and ways of thinking live on and are celebrated by all who loved him.

*As a caregiver, I can use the opportunity of Father's Day to honor my father, my loved one's father or fatherhood, and any other fathers who are important in our shared lives.*

***" . . . you come to realize how dynamic living on a planet can be when you remember that we're on one. . . . Aki—Earth. I will walk her skin today attuned to her heartbeat, the feel of her thrumming against the soles of my feet."***

—Richard Wagamese

I like to imagine the earth cares for each one of us as it holds us and treats us to unimaginable and abundant moments of beauty. Some days, when I was worn down and weary from caregiving, it was the earth and its multiple gifts that sustained and lifted me. If possible, walk barefoot upon the earth and let the heartbeat of the earth enter you. That heartbeat has an energy that will heal and uplift.

Any kind of walking upon the earth can be done in this way, with a deep tactile listening. The earth offers many other gifts as well, if one looks around. Trees and plants and flowers and rivers and lakes and streams and animals—too many to name, really. When you are feeling the small wears and tears of caregiving, remember that the earth we live on is surrounding us with color-infused energy. We need only to pay attention to the way the earth accepts us as we are and gently beckons us into the light, especially on this day that is one of the most light-filled days of the year.

*The ground I walk on and the natural beauty and light I walk through are helping me on this journey. I will let them in today.*

## *June 22*

***"Your financial stability comes first. Create a budget for you and your loved one."***

—Lucy Lazarony

For all people everywhere, finances are a necessary part of life's puzzle. It can be a complicated one for caregivers. If you are lucky, your loved one was able to plan ahead and has enough money for their care. Even in this best-case scenario, it usually falls to a caregiver to deal with financial transactions, bills, etc. In our family, due to our size and a variety of skill sets, there were two brothers who took over our mother's finances, which was enormously helpful. It is vital to assign this task to a trustworthy family member or to find a trusting person you can hire to do it.

Some caregivers end up helping financially, and this is a difficult and complicated path. Above all, it is recommended to never put one's own financial health in jeopardy. Just as putting our physical health in jeopardy renders us ineffective as caregivers, the same is true for financial health. There are people who specialize in these financial dilemmas and are well-acquainted with services available for your loved one. Long before you give up your own financial health, check out the resources available around you.

*Paying attention to money matters is part of the overall puzzle; it's important to look at and for all the pieces and find ways to make them fit.*

## *June 23*

***"Blessed are they who know that my ears today***
***May strain to catch the things they say."***

—Esther Mary Walker, *Beatitudes for Friends of the Aged*

Hearing loss is a common component of bodies that are wearing out due to age or other health problems. Communicating with someone who has hearing loss can be frustrating, but not nearly as frustrating as it is for those who have trouble hearing. One friend told me it's like living inside of a muffled tunnel. Many withdraw; many give up on communicating—thus, feeling lonely or isolated is all too common.

Many of us caregivers need to be especially sensitive about this issue. Slowing down as we talk (without talking down to them), and face-to-face communication can help a lot. By paying attention, we can make sure they heard what was said if there is a group conversation going on. We can cultivate a subtle sensitivity that will make a big difference in fostering a sense of belonging for our loved one. Such sensitivity is rooted in empathy.

*May the blessing of empathy always help me find sensitive and creative ways to communicate with my loved one in spite of their hearing loss.*

## *June 24*

**"Caregiving requires breaks, so we can fill the tank and replenish the soul."**

—Rev. Dr. Paul C. Hayes

Although it seems obvious that a role as demanding as that of a caregiver would require breaks from the intensity, it is often much harder to truly honor. Since the needs are deep and often seemingly endless and most caregivers are busy people, it is all too easy to not schedule a break. Then one day, you realize how desperately you do need one.

Since caregiving can be draining and it does tap into deep soul work (the work of love), we need ways to refill when feeling drained, or ideally before feeling drained. We need ways to keep our soul replenished. It is most ideal to have a regular way to take a break, in order to continually refill the tank of our energy. Breaks can come in large and small ways; each of us needs to know how to best replenish ourselves. Each of us needs to remember that the job itself requires us to take that break—to replenish the best of who we are.

*Today I will make a plan to take a break—*
*the kind of break that most replenishes*
*my energy and ability to love.*

## *June 25*

***"Music replays the past memories, awakens our forgotten worlds and makes our minds travel."***

—Michael Bassey Johnson

There are probably forms of music or songs that are particular to your family. In my family, the Irish sing-along songs were favorites over long periods of time. So when my uncle's congestive heart failure severely limited his ability to move about in the world, I always knew that if I sat at the piano and played a couple of the old favorites, he would brighten up—and often sing.

The same was true for my father and mother. I felt lucky to have this ability to bring them the music they had known and loved for decades of their lives. At times when a piano was not available, there was always the human voice or a recording on a phone. The father of a good friend was a lover of jazz—she recorded some of his favorite musicians, and he often drifted off to sleep at night listening to it.

*Music is often a great way to feel less alone. It's a gift I can find a way to provide for my loved one.*

## *June 26*

**"Advance directives need to be in writing. Depending on where you live, a form may need to be signed by a witness or notarized. You can ask a lawyer to help you with the process, but it is generally not necessary."**

—Mayoclinic.org

Since death can come at any time to any of us, the filling out of advance directives is important and helpful for all. But it is especially important for caregivers and their loved ones to talk about, to discuss what the loved one wants and to put it in writing. It's important to know exactly where these forms are and to have them handy. We actually had on my mother's refrigerator a signed and notarized copy of her desires for DNI and DNR.

Although not a nurse like my sister, I became very familiar with these terms—do not resuscitate, do not intubate. Signed by our mother. When these wishes are not talked about and clarified ahead of time, a crisis is often very difficult and fraught with differences of opinion. Such a conversation may be difficult, as end of life is a hard reality to look at, but ultimately it can be a healing and important conversation. An important component of caregiving is working things like this out with our loved one and letting the signed forms speak for themselves.

*I will honor the importance of having the paperwork handy for what my loved one wants when we reach the end of their life. It is another way to honor and respect who they are.*

*June 27*

***"He (my father) always understood that life is short and one's place in the world is small. But he also saw himself as a link in a chain of history . . . My father had helped us see that he was part of a story going back thousands of years—and so were we."***

—Atul Gawande

Perhaps because caregiving is so often about being with someone who is preparing for the end of their lives, it provides us all with a chance to think about intergenerational time. To ponder connections to ancestors who came long before us. It gives us time to ponder truths that are passed, like electrical currents, through threads of time.

The idea of being a link in a chain invites us all to be the best link we can be. And since all else dissipates, the most enduring link has to be love. We practice that loving link as we provide care for our loved one and model that for any future generations around us.

*Today I will take into deep consideration how my loved one and myself are links in a chain of history. I want to be the link of love.*

## *June 28*

***"Nothing that happens is to be ignored. Everything requires attention and mindfulness. There are spiritual gems to be recovered from the difficult challenges."***

—Rabbi Yehudah Fine

I love the concept of "spiritual gems." Since a gem is small, it is easily overlooked, covered up, misplaced. But when it is found and held in the light, it transforms into a thing of beauty. Gems can be said to glow from within or to catch any surrounding light and refract and reflect it.

Inside the difficult challenges of caregiving are many buried gems. There are gems of compassion and of tenderness, of connecting with others who understand the deep feelings that are part of this journey. There are occasional gems of intimacy in new and unexpected ways between you and your loved one. Allow these moments to shine as the moonstones, emeralds, and diamonds that they are.

*Attention to the gems I am experiencing amidst the hard moments is a way to polish and shine and honor today's particular beauty.*

## *June 29*

***"We must not see any person as an abstraction. Instead, we must see in every person a universe with its own secrets, with its own treasures, with its own sources of anguish, and with some measure of triumph."***

—Elie Wiesel

There were definitely times I felt impatient with my mother. From what I have observed, this is not uncommon. People's personalities often become more pronounced as they age and/or suffer. When caregiving feels more like a chore, it's time to remember the fullness of the human being we are caring for. Beyond an aggravating character trait is a full and rich human being. Within all of our loved ones are unspoken pains and quiet treasures.

The more we remember the fullness of our loved ones, the more we deepen into an appreciation for whom we are caring. The true challenge of caregiving is to always find our way back to a full appreciation and respect for all that lives inside of them. They may be currently limited in expression, but the more we find ways to appreciate the fullness of who they have been, the more we deliver care respectfully. Letting go of our own impatience is part of this.

*Help me to remember that inside of my loved one is a full universe filled with a spectrum from anguish to triumph.*

## *June 30*

***"Hear me! A single twig breaks, but the bundle of twigs is strong."***

—Tecumseh, Shawnee, 1795

No one of us can do this job alone, nor could our loved one thrive in any way if left alone to figure it all out. This beautiful image from the natural world reminds us of the strength to be found in community. Together, our hearts and hands can find strength during times of doubt, uncertainty, setbacks, and the slow diminishing of life energy. None of these challenges are for the faint of heart.

Alone we might be broken, blown away. But even the support of a few key people can help us become the bundle that stays strong. It's a basic life lesson and one that makes a key difference for those of us who are caregiving. One good friend who knows what we are going through is enormously helpful. A support group is another way to find essential support. The string tying the bundle of twigs together is the interweaving of community. Your support team helps you, you help support your loved one, your loved one returns support to you in myriad ways. On and on the essential and beautiful interweaving goes.

*Hear! Hear! This is a day to honor the community of support around me, to honor how we are all stronger together than we are alone.*

# July

## *July 1*

***"I miss my Dad every day. I wish I had felt less burdened during his last months."***

—Darcy Gibson Berglund

Most of us, after our loved one leaves this world, wish we had been more compassionate or more generous—not less so. For those in the trenches as you read this, it's a message to take to heart. When reflecting back, I see how sometimes a cultural or familial lack of appreciation for the job of caregiving underpinned those moments. Also, at times the reality of many needs in my life and a shortage of time played a role in that feeling of burden.

The more I talk with others and read about the journey of caregiving, the deeper my respect grows for this life path. One hears the words "mindfulness" and "compassion" more and more these days, an inspiring trend. Caregiving is a daily invitation into both of those practices. By showing up and doing so with love and kindness in your heart, you are developing yourself as a spiritual person, whatever that means to you. It's an opportunity to fully embrace.

*Today I will cherish the simple gift of being here with and for my loved person; I know I will miss her/him/them when that time comes.*

## *July 2*

***"Be faithful in small things because it is in them that your strength lies."***

—Mother Teresa

If we are viewing our days from a big-picture perspective, we might know that it is the accumulation of small gestures that matters over time. Still, it is easy to lose this awareness. I am often struck at funerals by how seldom we speak of huge accomplishments but rather a person's interests, kindnesses, and small gestures over time that reflected a life that touched others.

Yet we often get buried in the many small needs of caregiving. The small needs can feel simultaneously overwhelming and also perhaps unimportant in some larger sense. And yet, we need to remind ourselves that the small things are really what life is ultimately all about. The small consistencies—a listening ear, the reminder of the doctor appointment, simple companionship—are the core strengths we bring as a caregiver to our loved one. Over and over again.

*Today I will notice a small gesture or two on my part and honor their importance. They are part of the strength I bring to and share on this journey.*

## *July 3*

***"Stay fluid and roll with those changes. Life is just a big extended improvisation."***

—Jane Lynch

There are some grace periods in the caregiving world, when things can settle into a peaceful rhythm, when the schedule is working well for you as the caregiver. But there are also times of chaos and disruption—falls happen, the flu happens, pneumonia happens. Everyone scrambles—what needs to happen next?

It's easy to feel resentful and/or anxious. The disruption of course affects your life. The more you can creatively improvise and roll with the changes, the less stressful it will be for you. The above quote is from an actor—think of how people improvise on stage or do ad libs. In this case, you have been given a (forced) opportunity to practice improvisation, to practice the spiritual skills of emotional flexibility, of creative solutions. These skills will help you through the immediate crisis but will also deepen your response to changes for the rest of your life.

*When changes are happening with my loved one, I can adapt and find solutions because I am good at improvising and am learning how to stay fluid and roll with what is happening. Such challenges are workout exercises for my spiritual well-being.*

## *July 4*

***"Time and reflection change the sight little by little, till we come to understand."***

—Paul Cezanne

Caregiving is often so demanding that there are swirls of emotions we don't really have time to fully absorb or honor with our attention. Sometimes our view is skewed by the intensity of caring for a loved one and often watching him or her suffer in some way. There were days when it was hard for me, inside this intensity, to understand why some of my siblings were less engaged than I was. I also imagined that they questioned what I was doing and why.

I remember the hospice social worker talking to all of us about how everyone has their own unique way of dealing with grief, of processing and expressing it. At times, this was difficult for me, my judgmental nature struggled with it. In hindsight, I can see how each of my siblings cared for my mom in their own special way—even if occasional, their gestures mattered to her. And I am deeply grateful I was close to her for this journey, not an infrequent visitor.

*Today I will remember that it is a gift to myself to be a caregiver, to be a companion to this loved one as he or she inches her/his way out of this precious world. Other, more conflicted feelings will one day find their resolution.*

## *July 5*

***"This is an important lesson to remember when you're having a bad day, a bad month, or a sh***y year. Things will change; you won't feel this way forever. And anyway, sometimes the hardest lessons to learn are the ones your soul needs most."***

—Kelly Cutrone

Near the end of my mother's life, during a time of lots of ups and downs, she could one day look near death's door and the next seem sprightly and able. The sheer up and down-ness was exhausting at times. Out for coffee with friends, I found myself saying, "This is the hardest thing I have ever done." In the moment, it felt true. But it was mostly hard because I was tired and because it had gone on for a long time.

Fortunately, after a night of sleep and after sharing my feelings, I was able to get fully back on board for my mother's remaining days. I am so grateful for that. As long and enduring as the road to her death felt at times, now that it is over, I see how fleeting it was. To my tired self back then, I say, it really is so temporary. Do whatever it takes to rejuvenate yourself and get back to your commitment to care. It is so worthwhile.

*Hard days and exhaustion are a part of caregiving. The most meaningful thing I can do is rejuvenate myself for the next day, stay on track in the big-picture way, and know this time is both fleeting and important.*

# *July 6*

***"Love can change a person the way a parent can change a baby—awkwardly and often with a great deal of mess."***

—Lemony Snicket

My sister and I were the primary caregivers for my mother in her last years and particularly in her last months. My sister is a nurse, so a natural caregiver, and was always close to our mother. I had a more fragmented relationship with my mother. For long periods of time, in my youth and early adulthood, we bumped up against each other. I often, I am ashamed to admit, felt disdain toward her.

Of course, much changes over time. As I matured and deepened, I began to see my mother in a much wider lens and in a much more compassionate and generous way, long before her physical demise. This paved the way for me to want to be there to care for her. And those days and years of caring were my way of making amends for my earlier years of a hardened heart toward her. Those days of caring for her were melting the last edges of hardness in my heart toward my mother, who had given me the gift of life. Even as I wrestled with exhaustion, guilt, or even on some days, irritation, all along I felt the pulse of this spiritual gift of making amends and softening previously hard edges of my heart.

*I will be grateful today for the opportunity to rewrite the script of my relationship with my loved one, to find healing where there used to be hurt.*

## July 7

***"It's not that I believe everything happens for a reason... It's just that...I just think that some things are meant to be broken. Imperfect. Chaotic. It's the universe's way of providing contrast, you know? There have to be a few holes in the road. It's how life is."***

—Sarah Dessen

Bodies break down. Brains get rustier. Teeth wear out. When you are a caregiver, you have a heightened awareness of brokenness. You are watching it, living with it in so many ways. We come into this world as vulnerable and needy beings, and for many, this is also how we get ready to leave this world. Although every situation is unique, there is a natural order to this brokenness.

As caregivers we are, above all, witnesses to the brokenness. Companions. Advocates. So often there is nothing that can be done, but where we can step in and advocate for the best care, that is so important and vital. When we can hold a hand as bad news is delivered, or rub an aching body part, or hang a happy picture on the wall, we are mending the hole as best we can. Since witnessing brokenness takes its toll, it is so important to have support on this journey, someone who supports and comforts and encourages you as you walk this caregiving path.

*It's how life is—it breaks down. As I watch this in my loved one and provide a healing presence as I can, I will also reach out for support for my own emotional needs and broken edges.*

## *July 8*

***"The art of life is a constant readjustment to our surroundings."***

—Kakuzo Okakura

When a loved one is dealing with a health or aging crisis, adjustments are part of the journey. They are adjusting to physical problems that arise, and often there are adjustments that have to do with living space, personnel, new health protocols, etc. As a caregiver, you are adjusting to their adjustments. Sometimes, I felt like a juggler in the circus, with a new ball being thrown at me just as I was getting used to juggling three balls—lopsided balls, balls arriving out of some peripheral no man's land that I didn't see coming.

Caregiving is a kind of circus act, a high-wire balance. In this way, it is an exercise in living an artful life. How do you juggle those multiple balls, how do you keep your balance when you feel like you are hanging out over unknown territory? When too many balls are coming at you, how do you find a graceful way to take a break from juggling, how do you pare it down to the three manageable balls you can juggle this day, leaving the rest to be dealt with another day?

*The challenge of my day is to hone the art of living fully inside of today—juggling what I can and letting go of the rest, seeking balance as I walk the tightrope of my caregiving journey.*

## *July 9*

***"Life requires of man (and woman) spiritual elasticity, so that he may temper his (her) efforts to the chances that are offered."***

—Victor Frankl

Caregiving can require so many skills that it is often mind-boggling. A caregiver is nurse, nurturer, advocate, clothing shopper, errand-runner, disseminator of information to family and health personnel, and more. Whew, it is quite a list. It's a juggling act—one that requires, inspires, and offers opportunities to develop spiritual elasticity. It is a spiritual path, so it is most helpful to look toward whatever your spiritual beliefs or practices are for guidance. Let your view of the spiritual life encourage you to do what you need to do today. Let it underscore the deep soul work you are doing—for your own soul, as you comfort your loved one through these vulnerable days.

Caregiving gives us a close and intimate look at how vulnerable all of us human beings are. There is tenderness here and authentic connection. The tenderness of holding hands, of quiet conversation, of just listening or sharing the details of a hard day. There is room here for give and take, for the flow of spirit to arrive in subtle and surprising ways.

*Today I will practice spiritual elasticity as I listen and deeply respond to the challenges in front of me.*

## *July 10*

***"In the distance a sparrow is singing over and over his serene and very simple song. . . . on and on, the sparrow sings."***

—Mary Oliver

Nature provides many ways to find comfort and rejuvenation. Sometimes I needed to be reminded of this simple possibility, especially on days when I felt mired in details as a caregiver. Besides feeling the tugs of time, there is often the difficulty of balancing other commitments. There can be complications of all sorts—with medications, with other people caring for your loved one, with new needs or new diagnoses.

When one feels overwhelmed, take a few moments to enter into whatever natural elements surround you. Perhaps it is stopping to listen to the serene melody of a nearby bird. Perhaps it is taking a few moments to watch the sun go down and splay its magical colors across the sky. Perhaps it is picking up a leaf from the ground and smelling it and noticing its colors. Nature provides healing beauty, and it is always there for you. If possible, share the leaf or the moonrise with your loved one. If that isn't possible, breathe in deep the comfort of the eternal and yet fleeting beauty of the world around you.

*I will find a few moments today to let the natural world comfort and uplift me and rejuvenate my soul.*

## *July 11*

***"The healthy, the strong individual is the one who asks for help when he (she) needs it, whether for an abscess on his knee or in her soul."***

—Rona Barrett

A friend of mine took care of her husband for years before he passed away. She gave up working out, gave up getting together with friends. Her world grew smaller and smaller. After his death, it took her many months and even years to recover her physical strength and stamina. In retrospect, she says, she wishes she would have claimed some regular self-care time. In hindsight, a couple of hours away from caregiving would not have made his life any less comfortable or meaningful, but it would have made a big difference in her life.

This corresponds to stories of caregivers who die before their loved ones do—or get sick and are unable to carry on with the caregiving their loved ones need. It is such a delicate balance, and yet, the statistics show that the most effective caregivers are those who are able to find a way to take care of their own needs along the way. Asking for help is imperative, so is having your own support system who cheer you on both in your commitment to caregiving but also to devoting some time to your own needs.

*Asking for help or for support to take care of myself is not a sign of weakness or failure on my part; rather, it is a sign of strength and self-awareness. I am a more effective and loving caregiver when I am finding ways to take care of myself along the way.*

## *July 12*

***"Are you a caregiver? Do you have caregiver stress?"***

—Health questionnaire form

Many medical health questionnaires include the above questions. Health professionals are seeing the potential negative impact that caregiver stress can have on the caregiver's health. This is such an important statement about the reality of the hazards of caregiving. It is crucial to find ways to take care of one's own needs. This is a tricky, complex balance and one that often changes from day to day. Often the needs of our loved one seem so bottomless that one feels guilty about setting a boundary or carving out the time for some self-care. But doing so is essential. Doing so in a spirit of love is especially essential.

A burned-out caregiver often gets sick, is irritable, or even gets angry in a way that doesn't feel good to anyone. Your body will tell you when you are walking this precipice, when the balance needs to shift to paying attention to yourself—for an hour, an afternoon, perhaps a weekend break. Loving yourself in this way ultimately deepens your ability to give care to your loved one—it's a vital practice.

*Today I will honor my own need for care in a concrete way—perhaps a candlelit bath, a long walk on a favorite trail, or dinner with an old friend.*

## *July 13*

***"If I'd known I was going to live this long, I'd have taken better care of myself."***

—Jimmy Durante

Although the above quote was spoken with humor, there is nothing funny about taking care of someone who has, to a certain extent or in some way, not taken care of themselves. It is like you are left holding the baggage of their choices. This is a particularly difficult path, and it requires some soul-searching about why you have taken on this role. Perhaps it's to help out another loved one, to be part of a team of caregivers. Perhaps it's a deeply rooted sense of duty. Perhaps it's to honor the history or family legacy you share with this person. Perhaps it's because there is no one else and you can't quite live with no one advocating for this person.

All are valid reasons. And perhaps all of us caregivers fall into one or more of these categories on any given day, depending on our own state of mind. But taking care of someone who hasn't or doesn't take very good care of themselves requires a huge degree of letting go of what one can't control or change and systematic ways to keep clarifying our own purpose and vision. Some resentment is only human, but if it becomes an overriding feeling around giving care, it becomes toxic. We all owe it to ourselves to find ways to give care from a more centered and spiritual place than resentment. All of us called to this journey have the heart-opening capacity to do so.

*Today I will renew my vows as a caregiver and re-center myself around all the right reasons I chose this role—right for me, right for my soul, right for my path through this life and time.*

## *July 14*

***"The greatest healing therapy is friendship and love."***

—Hubert Humphrey

Friendship and love do stretch our ability to feel joy and help lighten the load of our burdens. What you are ultimately providing for a loved one is this gift. Yes, it gets disguised under the many other functions of the job. It really belongs at the top of the list. You are loving your loved one through a very difficult time in his or her life. You are holding her hand through it, making it a little less lonely. And that kind of sharing works two ways. My mother and I became much deeper friends on this journey. I know it doesn't always work that way, but her vulnerable self was often easy to love as long as I didn't let it overwhelm me. As long as I didn't feel like I needed to "fix" it. Or rather, as long as I didn't feel guilty about not meeting her every need.

I could be a true friend and love her. I did. And I was better at this when I deeply knew that I deserved the same kind of support, in most likely a slightly different way. I really needed to know I could talk to my friends or my caregiving sister when I was feeling down or overwhelmed. I wouldn't have been able to hang in there as truly as I did if it hadn't been for my own resources of love and friendship. An understanding spouse or friend or family member is invaluable.

*Today I will both provide love and friendship and seek it in my own heart.*

## *July 15*

***"It is this intangible thing, love in its many forms, which enters into every therapeutic relationship. . . . And it is an element which binds and heals, which comforts and restores, which works what we have to call—for now—miracles."***

—Karl Menninger

Over the long years of my relationship with my mother, we often had a hard time meeting on common ground. One of the treasures of our time together in the last years of her life was the moments we fell into honest conversation, where she spoke openly of something she had held inside of her so many years. It was like watching a flower bloom or studying the beautiful underside of a multi-veined leaf. Such moments were gifts, for they shed light on the history we had shared and gave me a greater understanding of who she was and what she had been through.

This, in turn, touched me and shed light into my own heart. Being there and listening deeply helped to create these special moments. They are surrounded by a special light in my memory.

*As intangible and subtle as they may be, there are gifts coming my way as I show up to care for my loved one. I will listen closely and appreciate what comes my way.*

## *July 16*

***"A happy life is made up of little things . . . a gift sent, a letter written, a call made, a recommendation given, transportation provided, a cake made . . . "***

—Carol Holmes

We live in a world of multiple expectations, where we are often encouraged to reach for more and to strive for our dreams. When one is struggling with an illness or just slowing down as a natural progression of age, the focus changes. Slows down. Enters more into the realm of enjoying the moment, finding a helpful way to get through a day, rather than striving for big accomplishments. Often the days when I helped my Mom write special cards to an old friend or one of her grandchildren or helped her organize a small gift for her neighbor made us both happy. Small moments, small gestures gave us both a sense of satisfaction.

Often it was reaching out to someone we both cared about beyond the two of us. It was a way to expand our circle of care. Those days were reminders to me of the importance of small gestures of caring—so easy to forget in my busyness.

*The slowing down that is part of spending time with my loved one is often a gift in disguise—an opportunity to remind myself of the simple gestures that enhance a loving life.*

## *July 17*

***"Those who expect moments of change to be comfortable and free of conflict have not learned their history."***

—Joan Wallach Scott

Change is always hard and seems to be a regular part of caring for a loved one. For one thing, the vulnerable are more at risk. For another, the vulnerable tend to be less able to adapt on their own. It seemed to my sister and I, as we walked so closely with our mother through her last months, that something was always shifting. There were falls, sicknesses, medication adjustments, and changes in personnel that were hard for our mother. We made requests to our siblings for extra help from time to time. Sometimes we needed to hire extra help.

These times were often fraught with differing opinions or a shortage of information about finances or medical vulnerabilities. Sometimes we felt like we were overreacting . . . or we wondered if others were underreacting. Care meetings were often helpful but never easy. Every new problem or decision seemed to have a ripple effect that required further adjustment. This never meant someone was doing something wrong—only that there were multiple ways of trying to figure out a complex problem. It seemed most helpful to accept this rather than to fight it and to realize that, most of the time, everyone involved was doing the best they could.

*I can accept that the decision-making process will not always be smooth, that there will be some misunderstandings on our way to finding the right next decision. But together, we can figure out how to best get through times of change.*

## *July 18*

***"Most of us, in fact, have had the experience of opening a family album and being filled with a sense of the past which is suddenly there, a part of our present reality."***

—Jane Taylor McDonnell

One day when my mother was feeling a little blue, we pulled out a family album that contained pictures of holiday celebrations from over the years. It actually contained pictures from over a ten-year period from a time when our mother was active and healthy and fully able to travel, drive, and move from place to place. Going through those photos was a touchstone to an easier time in her life. We laughed about some of the facial expressions and fashion choices (glasses!) from over the years. We commented on how everyone looked younger and thinner and how such cute toddlers and kids grew into handsome adults.

The afternoon was brightened by the light of the past. Whether you spend time over one important photo or have some organized in an album, sharing photos can be a heartwarming way to spend time with your loved one. In some inexplicable way, time disappears. The past is right here in the present moment, filling it with years' worth of memories, of shared experiences inside this mystery called life.

*The next time I am able, I will use a photo or photos of a happier time to light up my loved one's day and my own.*

***"The families that grow closer through their parents' care do so by communicating freely, shouldering burdens ungrudgingly, finding other ways to chip in when they can't be present, and by expressing gratitude for those doing the toughest work."***

—Carolyn Hax (advice columnist, *Star Tribune* 10/23/19)

The family component around caregiving is always an important one. If you are an only child, you carry a particularly lonely path caring for your parents, and I hope you have plenty of other forms of support—from a partner, a support group, or friends and/or professionals helping you. If you are not an only child—especially of the person you are caring for—then you have the blessing of other helping (hopefully) hands and the complexities of family dynamics.

Rarely is there a fair distribution around caregiving—so much depends on people's schedules, time of life as the crises hit, finances, and personality or willingness. A lot depends on the relationship each person has with the loved one who is failing. There is no right way to do this, but the quote above covers all the most important aspects of getting through such a time as an intact family. Talking to each other about what is going on, sharing information, finding creative ways to help if you can't be there, and above all, appreciating and thanking the ones doing the toughest work—all of these are key, especially the last one.

*I am grateful for being appreciated by my family members when they thank me. If they are unable to support me, I can find such appreciation from my support people and from others who understand just how tough this job can be.*

## *July 20*

**"Drill down farther, as the (AARP) studies do and it's evident that women—why would this surprise anyone?—carry a disproportionate burden."**

—Jane Gross

When I looked around at my fellow caregivers, they were often female. I remember talking to the assisted living director who said she had seen this to be the case in most situations. Not all: there are exceptions. But I do have five brothers, and although they often took care of other needs (financial, legal, etc.), the hands-on care was primarily done by my sisters and me.

At times, this was difficult for me. Yes, those demons of resentment and anger reared their heads. Those were challenging days. It was so important for me to have a few people who understood this. There was no time or energy to change the existing system. It was what it was. Most of those feelings have dissipated for me over time. I can appreciate now what everyone did do. And I cherish the memories I have of being there, really just being there, when my mother most needed it. So, the gift of how the system worked is that I had the opportunity to practice compassion many days and times with the woman who gave me the gift of life.

*In dividing up what needs to be done with other family members, I will do what I can to get beyond my anger or resentment. Letting that go, I can re-commit to my purpose of being a compassionate caregiver—it is truly who I want to be.*

## *July 21*

**"Special stones hold a spiritual power in my palm, often reminding me to be gentle with myself and the world around me."**

—Patricia Hoolihan, *journal*

Due to the emotional intensity of caregiving and its often-unrelenting demands, exhaustion is part of the path, at least from time to time, if not regularly. So when exhaustion arrives, find the stone in your home that is from a favorite place on earth. If you are lucky enough to be able to go walk near stones, granite, rocks, then all the better. But if you have done so in your life and brought back small stones as reminders of more expansive times, these can be more easily accessible.

Take a few moments with the stone in your hand and allow it to calm you. All stone is ancient; it has listened across time and accepted everything it has heard. Absorb this quiet, calm, listening and accepting kind of energy. Know that your tired bones are filled with love and need gentle tending—excessively gentle tending. There are many ways to do so, what is most important is shining the light of kindness and understanding upon ourselves. What is most important is an attitude of gentleness—a patient and deep gentleness.

*Stone energy reminds me today to be gentle with myself—to do what eases the hard edges of my tiredness, and to do so with a gentle generosity toward self.*

## *July 22*

***"When people experience deep suffering, what helps them most of all—more than anything we can say or do—is how we are. What matters most is love . . . to be present and listen is often all that it takes."***

—Kirsten DeLeo

There are going to be days when you are aware of the suffering of your loved one; sometimes it is physical pain or disappointing news of some sort. It is difficult to hold in one's heart, the suffering of a loved one. Often we get caught up in thinking we need to do something or fix it. We get caught up in worrying about the right thing to say.

If anything can be done to alleviate suffering, of course it is the right thing to set that in motion. Often, for people suffering from disease or physical crumbling due to aging, there is no fix. But know that your listening presence helps soften the edges of that hard experience. Being there, listening, can really and truly provide the healing a person needs.

*Rather than seeking a miracle cure, I will honor that my presence and my ability to listen to my loved one is a healing balm and truly, for today, makes a difference that matters.*

## *July 23*

***"The often long process of providing care for a loved one can take a toll on us as caregivers."***

—Barry Jacobs and Julia Mayer

Among my caregiving friends, we often say what a hard job it is—especially if it goes on and on. Exhaustion is more often than not a part of the journey. I remember thinking often of John Lennon's words, "I'm so tired, I haven't slept a wink," because sometimes the worry-gremlins kicked in at night also. So there's a tender balance to be struck between knowing the job can wear us down and knowing when we need to take a break and re-boot our caregiving selves.

For an always exhausted caregiver can often get sick and for sure runs low on the kind of energy that is most helpful. So part of the journey is honoring when you need to rejuvenate. Sometimes this can be done in short portions of time: take a long bath and go to bed early after a particularly challenging day. Take a day or weekend off—make arrangements for others to care for your loved one. Do something that reminds you of who you are at your best—take in music, walk a favorite wooded trail, visit the water that always comforts you.

*There are many ways to re-energize. I owe it to myself and my loved one to find ways to honor the tiring journey I am on and to revitalize myself for the next steps.*

## *July 24*

***"Mother finally says, 'I just want to listen to the silence with you by my side.' The fullness of silence. I am learning what this means."***

—Terry Tempest Williams

Years ago, I visited my beloved uncle at the well-known Mayo Clinic. He was being tested for heart problems. When I entered his room, he was alone and sleeping. I sat beside him, watching his chest rise and fall. I savored the peacefulness of his even breathing, I savored the reality that he was still breathing, I felt lulled by the quiet into long moments of gratitude. I was so grateful for him, for all the gifts he had shared with me in his lifetime.

When he woke, he cracked a joke about taking a "nipper-napper," and the day moved into a different mood. In the days to come, the news was not good, but many of us family members convened around him, and we all helped to collectively carry what was happening. Years later, those quiet moments with him still come back to me, as precious as rays of light breaking through clouds.

*When the moments present themselves, I can settle into the gift of the fullness of shared silence with my loved one, or even with myself.*

## *July 25*

***"A sense of humor . . . is needed armor. Joy in one's heart and some laughter on one's lips is a sign that the person down deep has a pretty good grasp of life."***

—Hugh Sidey

Technology has been and can be a real asset, as we have learned during COVID-19. It's a great tool to employ as a caregiver, especially as a tool for humor or joy. If you are able to visit or be with your loved one, you can bring in short clips on your phone or laptop of a comedian or a posted video of a child dancing, of a bird hatching out of its shell. Pure magic! Much is available online in this way. If your loved one does email or texting, you can send short humorous clips or photos and videos that capture small moments of joy.

The act of shared laughter doubles the appreciation of humor and deepens the momentary sense of joy. As caregivers, it is so helpful to tune into what brings laughter or joy to our loved one. Often it is very simple and easily available. In my family, we often re-played a video for my father of his two-year-old-great grandson singing Happy Birthday, which sounded a lot more like Happy Doo Doo and was charming beyond the words I have to describe it. This never failed to bring mirth to my father's eyes and a smile to his face.

*Humor and quiet joy often go together; sharing such moments with our loved ones brightens the day all the way around.*

## *July 26*

**"No mud. No lotus."**

—Thich Nhat Hanh

Every blossom in the world emerges from the darkness of earth and mud. Mud is messy; when we walk through it, we leave tracks behind us. Often what is germinating in the mud is invisible to us for a time until it emerges.

Muddy experiences around caregiving are part of the experience. Not knowing what is ahead is akin to a muddy, murky process. Bumping into our own inadequacies can be akin to walking in mud; our quick temper or rush to judgment leaves tracks behind us that sometimes call for cleaning up. All of this is part of the rich soil that nourishes the blossoming of love in a dark time. We clear the air between us and our loved ones, we take steps inside of uncertain times, and what emerges is a new petal on the flower of love. The lotus blooms; its scent sweetens the air.

*I can accept that muddy moments, where nothing feels clear, are part of what nourishes, always, the flowering love between me and my loved one.*

## *July 27*

**"What we don't need in the midst of struggle is shame for being human."**

—Brene Brown

Repeatedly, I remember the times when I felt overwhelmed as a caregiver. I felt exhausted; in those moments, I questioned my strength for the journey. In some moments, I wished for it to be over. It always helped to say this to a trusted other person or to write it in my journal. Both were ways to accept what was difficult to look at or speak aloud and then begin to move forward. Those moments were not my shining ones, and it would have been easy to feel shame about them. In fact, at times I did feel shame.

Shame is like a dark cloth over the human experience. Once removed, we can see our frailties as part of our being human. Life is hard enough, especially life as a caregiver, without adding the weight of shame to the experience. If you, like I did, find yourself thinking unkind and harsh thoughts, find a way to embrace your humanness. Awareness is the first step, and then granting oneself permission to be imperfectly human. Acceptance will open the door to moving on to being kinder to both yourself and your loved one.

*As a caregiver, I will be given many an opportunity to accept my humanness: this is humbling and also the most reliable route back to honoring my better self.*

## *July 28*

***"Blessed are they who never say,***
***'you've told that story twice today.'"***

—Esther Mary Walker, *Beatitudes for Friends of the Aged*

Many people who don't have any specific memory issues repeat their stories. It's common. But it is especially common among older people and, of course, is a hallmark of many kinds of memory loss. Stories that get repeated are often told because they contain meaning for the storyteller. It's not easy to be at the receiving end of repeated stories; sometimes it's concerning or just plain boring.

One of my brothers has a message on his phone machine that says, "It is what it is." It's a helpful mantra in the face of memory loss, inside the moment of hearing a certain story again. Acceptance of life's absurdities can go a long way, especially if lined with a quiet sense of humor.

*May the blessings of acceptance and humor help me today as I listen to that story that seems to want to be told—again.*

## *July 29*

***"Self-care is giving the world the best of you, not what's left of you."***

—Katie Reed

There were definitely days in my caregiving world where I felt wrung out, empty. Sometimes, if no one else was available or if there was an emergency need, I simply had to dig deep and summon the needed energy. But other days, there was a choice. And many a time, I noticed that if I took time to nurture or nourish myself, I became a much more centered and loving person and caregiver.

Often just taking time for my favorite walk before or after I visited my mother made a big difference for me. Sitting once in a while in a coffee shop with my journal both relaxed and re-energized me. Lighting a candle in the morning as I savored my first sips of coffee. Carving out these moments and looking forward to them helped keep my sense of self from being too depleted. Also, when emotions were filling up and spilling over, it was essential to talk them through with my friends who understood.

*I am a better caregiver when I carve out some time to take a break, to care for my own needs. I want to give from a full heart, not an empty one.*

## *July 30*

***"If I could distill all the great writings on suffering down to a few words, I would simply say that suffering and crisis transform us, humble us, and bring out what matters most in life."***

—Rabbi Yehudah Fine

Caregiver support groups are places where we can find fellow travelers who are experiencing similar challenges. Many churches and community groups and medical clinics provide such support. They are really worth tracking down. But if not available, it is helpful to have a few people supporting you on this path. Something particularly helpful is to focus once in a while on what you are learning.

Caring for a loved one through times of crisis and suffering does indeed transform and humble us. We become more aware of the fragility of life and that inside this fragility we are invited to love more deeply and to cherish more completely our time together on this planet. Finding people and places where we can talk about this, and honor these learnings, deepens our sense of meaning and helps us remember what really matters.

*At my fingertips, as I work my way through this time, is a daily reminder of what really matters in this life. The right kind of support will help me to see and honor this.*

## *July 31*

**"Love is the voice beneath all silences."**

—ee cummings

Some of my favorite moments with my mother were when she would drop off to sleep during my visit. Sometimes I would leave before that happened. But if she was not feeling well, or if we were waiting for an appointment or something, I just stayed. Into the peacefulness of her rhythmic sleeping came a moment of relief, of just being together. I remember checking in on other loved ones too when they were napping and absorbing the peacefulness of their breath, rising and falling in their frail chests.

There were other times when words failed me or when a silence fell at the end of all that needed to be said. Silence can make us uncomfortable, but learning to navigate and honor the love that lies beneath silence between loved ones is the true voyage. I am still grateful for those quiet moments when listening to the gift of breathing carried all the currents and force of love.

*I can accept and listen to the love flowing beneath any silence, which is part of my journey these days with my loved one.*

# August

## *August 1*

***"The Infinite Goodness has such wide arms that it takes whatever turns to it."***

—Dante Alighieri

I recently read how one cannot worry and pray at the same time. There is so much to worry about on the caregiving journey; often there is pain, discomfort, fear, or suffering in our loved one which is hard to witness and bear. There are so many unknowns, and uncertainty is difficult for most of us.

Whatever our belief systems around God or Higher Power may be, it is a larger sense of meaning that will bring us comfort in the dark moments. There can be enormous relief in turning our worries over to something greater, more benevolent, and understanding than our mortal and individual selves. I love the idea of the Infinite Goodness, so named by Dante in the 1700s. Across time, this image comes to those of us who are in need.

*When life feels like too much to bear, I will turn to those wide-open arms; a timeless force of Infinite Goodness will hold its arms open for me today.*

## *August 2*

**"Comparison is a death knell to sibling harmony."**

—Elizabeth Fishel

Overall, I felt very fortunate to have siblings through this process. Two of my brothers helped Mom with her finances, others set up regular or irregular times to visit her. Some sent flowers from afar. I always felt empathy for caregivers I knew who were only children—so much of all such responsibilities fall on their shoulders.

So the sharing helped. But it would be disingenuous of me to say that I didn't compare some days what I was doing and notice how much "less" others were doing. At times, this and other elements made our mother's journey very hard on the sibling relationships. There was really no way for it to be equal for reasons way too numerous to name. Ultimately, over and over again, I needed to accept what was, to ask for help when I needed it, and to take responsibility for my own choices. And, occasionally I needed to process my own feelings about it all with a trusted non-family friend.

*It can be a challenge to protect sibling harmony as we all watch and help our loved one go through a difficult time, but as a caregiver, I can ask for help when it is needed. I can accept my own choices gracefully.*

## *August 3*

***"The great thing about getting older is that you don't lose all the other ages you've been."***

—Madeleine L'Engle

When caring for a loved one who is sick or aging, we become easily and sadly focused on their shrinking skills and abilities. It's inevitable. Yet, it is essential to remember that living inside of them, somewhere and somehow, are all the previous selves they used to be. Sometimes my mother reminisced about her childhood days. Sometimes my father made reference to his war experiences. My friend whose mother has Alzheimer's says that some days her mother is talking to a dear childhood friend.

Keeping that in mind deepens our awareness of this mystery of life. Our own feelings from the past about the person we are caring for may also need attention along this journey. At times, I had had a difficult history with both of my parents. It was a mysterious blessing to be present for them during their vulnerabilities of aging and health problems—and an unexpected opportunity to gently heal our relationships.

*Along this path, I can quietly honor who my loved one has been at different times by being present to his or her full human complexity and to my own.*

## *August 4*

***"And in the end, the love you take is equal to the love you make."***

—Paul McCartney

I and many others have always loved these lyrics from one of the great musicians and musical groups of our time. These words boil down the essence of what it means to be in this world and what is most important in our connections with each other. Love is something we feel in our hearts, but it is expressed in a multitude of ways. We create love in our world by showing up when people are in need, showing up to celebrate life's important moments, sharing quiet cups of tea, helping to carry the weight of bad news.

Love is expressed when we help each other through the hard times and when we understand each other's fears. When we balance it with self-love, our gestures of love as a caregiver are building our own deep well of love. It's something we give and receive at the same time. In the end, it is what matters most.

*Caregiving is, above all, a path of love and one that nourishes my own well of love.*

## *August 5*

***" . . . boundaries and reciprocity are essential elements of caring practice, not signs of a lack of compassion."***

—Tove Pettersen

A healthy caring practice balances the needs of the day with an awareness of being able to care in a long-term way as well. As much as possible, it cares for one's own needs as well as the needs of our more vulnerable loved one. In other words, the need to set boundaries is not something to be twisted over with guilt; it is a necessary aspect of caring in a healthy way.

The need to take a break, to take a trip, or to take a day off to tend to other needs are all perfectly acceptable ways of being a full human being who is also a caregiver. Essential to being a truly caring caregiver is this ability to set boundaries. Also essential is an ability to receive from our loved one. The relationship, though it may seem unbalanced and is in some ways, is also a reciprocal one.

*It is healthy for me to set boundaries as I feel the need and to honor the emotional energy of both the burdens and gifts of caring for my loved one.*

## *August 6*

***"It [caregiving] gives us the opportunity to discover an inner capacity for kindness, compassion, and wisdom that we may never have suspected we possessed, even though it has always been ours."***

—Kirsten DeLeo

There were many years when I would not have been a likely choice to become a caregiver for my parents in their elder years. I was often rebellious, a questioner, someone who stirred up things. Most of us change and grow over the years, and gratefully, as I grew, I was able to see my parents from a larger and larger perspective.

It was an ongoing discovery for me to be the one who often showed up when things were going wrong with their health. We began to count on this, but it was never an obvious lifelong given. At one point, when my father was in the hospital, he was apologizing to me for causing so much "trouble." I answered that it is what we do for people we love and besides, I had given him some trouble over the years. "Oh that," he said. "That was nothing." A gift in that moment—absolution, forgiveness, amends. It was all there. Healing. Caregiving provides potential for this kind of healing, open spaces for compassion and wisdom we might not discover in any other way.

*Today I will honor what I am learning about myself, my better self, as I care for my loved one.*

## *August 7*

***"If you are blameful and bitter, may you be sweetened by hope and humor."***

—Elizabeth Lesser

As with most human beings, we caregivers have our bad days and our hopefully only occasional dips into bitterness. Things can go wrong. For many of us, there are probably professionals and other family members who are involved and sometimes throw things off-course. There are just plain circumstances that are often difficult and may incite us to casting blame.

Humor and hope can help turn these moments around. And communication—with all. It is hard to foresee all the needs for communication. One day, when my sister was out of town (on a break!), my mother was in a very anxious state because she could not find her jewelry box. We looked everywhere in her small apartment. Finally, I got on the phone and found out she had given it to my oldest brother for safekeeping, but forgot she had. It would have been nice to know that ahead of time, but communication did help us solve the problem. After she calmed down, we began to laugh. It was a much better outcome than some of the imagined worries we both had had.

*Although there may be moments of bitterness or blaming, we can move out of those moments through communication, through having a sense of humor, and through hope.*

## *August 8*

***"Heart of Mercy,***
***. . . Thank you for lovingly embracing me as I am***
***While the murky layers of my many shortcomings***
***Are slowly transformed into love."***

—Joyce Rupp

Caregiving is often such a many-faceted and enduring journey that we run into all of our own shortcomings. The job itself is one where it is all too easy to see how we fall short of all the possible needs and demands. Part of the ruggedness of the journey for me was how often I questioned myself, whether through guilt, a sense of inadequacy, or any number of other harsh self-judgments.

In those moments, I felt the need for mercy. The image of a heart of mercy that would embrace me and all of my shortcomings is a healing image. I particularly love the image of transforming those murky layers of self-questioning into love. It is a slow and deep process. As I turn it all over and into the arms of a heart of mercy, I realize how blessed I am to be on this caregiving path where I love deeply and daily, if imperfectly.

*As I grapple with my shortcomings, I can trust that they are slowly being transformed into love as I care for both myself and my loved one.*

## *August 9*

***"When we take one step after another, though at times we might fear becoming lost, we will eventually find our way home."***

—Stephen Levine

There are moments when caregiving is completely overwhelming. The emergency phone calls, the injury-rife falls, the refusal to eat, the mix-up of medications, the change of staff that has thrown our loved one off-balance. As caregivers, we want to pull our hair out or crumple into a weeping mess. It's a good idea to keep one's hair, but often a good cry is what clears our vision for the next step.

There are days when we might feel lost, or rather, that the way ahead is a wilderness with no clear trail, enshrouded in fog. Yet, even with fog, what is right in front of us is revealed as we step into it. Fear of what is ahead is our biggest obstacle. If we can just keep taking one step at a time, we will find our way.

*Although there are moments I feel lost on this caregiving trail, I am learning that if I just take the next step, the trail ahead will become more clear.*

## *August 10*

***"Trust your instincts, and make judgments on what your heart tells you. The heart will not betray you."***

—David Gemmell

Often, there are so many decisions to be made along this road—or the occasional really big ones. There's a lot to be said for doing one's research and asking questions, but ultimately many of these choices are best informed by our own instincts. This is especially true if one is making a decision about a care facility. Or about hiring extra help. Or about dialing in extra help if your loved one is at home.

As the caregiver, you have the best sense of who your loved one is and what their comfort level requires. So, ultimately, the person or place or medication need is something you have a real tangible sense about. Trust it. It's easy to doubt oneself, but keep listening to your inner, instinctive feeling about a decision. Courage is fear that has said its prayers.

*Today I will have the courage to listen to and to trust my instincts about a looming decision for my loved one.*

## *August 11*

***"Don't fool yourself and think that Spirit is somewhere else, in otherworldly experiences, in great rushes or ecstatic visions. Life's deepest experience is the joy that fills our hearts when we love and give to others."***

—Rabbi Yehudah Fine

It is so easy to fall into "the grass is greener on the other side" kind of thinking. Especially as caregivers. It is so easy to wish things were different, especially in the face of suffering or loss. But right here, embedded in this journey, is all that is most meaningful in life. When we can take an hour or an afternoon with our loved one and be fully present, we are making the most of this time.

In many ways, life's deepest experiences are right here in front of us each day that we are an active caregiver. And there is often a quiet joy here, the joy of companionship, of recognizing who we are to each other. Inside the quiet joy are many meaningful gestures of love.

*Today I will notice the small but meaningful connections between me and my loved one. By honoring those connections, I honor the spirit that is alive within me and between us always.*

## *August 12*

***"With all its sham, drudgery and broken dreams, it is still a beautiful world."***

—Desiderata

There are many broken dreams along the trails of life, especially as one ages or goes further into any kind of disease or physical frailty. And at times, the path of the caregiver can feel like drudgery, for its sheer repetition. Yet, embedded in this very old prayer is a reminder that in spite of life's difficulties, it is still a beautiful world. Truly it is.

So how do we remind ourselves of the beauty even if we are having a drudgery day? It's all in the looking for it. Beauty might be found in the broad and genuine smile and loving eyes of anyone around us. Beauty can be found in the song of the bird that wakes us early or sings from its perch in the late afternoon sun. Beauty is easily seen in flowers of all shapes and hues, in the deep colors of leaves on the tree we just walked or drove by.

*Beauty abounds; when we look for it, we can always find it. Beauty is a guiding light for my days as a caregiver.*

## *August 13*

**"A person without a sense of humor is like a wagon without springs. It's jolted by every pebble on the road."**

—Henry Ward Beecher

My father had a sense of humor that appreciated kids' antics, and many other of life's absurdities. The antics or word pronunciations of young children are often a good source of humor. If you are lucky enough to have some of those in the family, let them be the source of good humor. Some families have humorous stories that get told over and over again, or beloved humorous characters around whom those stories center. My uncle, who was a true eccentric, had funny ways of pronouncing certain words. He is long gone from this world, but my siblings and cousins and I still smile when we try to emulate his voice and pronunciations.

Being open to the humor around us, to the absurdities of life, can help us as we pull the wagon of our responsibilities over a rough road. The road is the same beneath us, but our ability to find buoyancy and resilience is expanded if we can share laughter as we go.

*Humor is around us, embedded in life's absurdities and in the eccentric and good-humored ways of children and other loved ones. Every pebble on a rough road can be softened by humor.*

## *August 14*

***"Patience is a form of wisdom. It demonstrates that we understand and accept the fact that sometimes things must unfold in their own time."***

—Jon Kabat-Zinn

There were long stretches with my mother when we knew she was on the edge of her ability to remain in assisted living or her ability to walk alone or her ability to withstand the pain in her body or . . . and the list could go on and on. Many days were shadowed by a sense of not knowing what was ahead or how the path would need to be cleared for what was ahead. Caregiving creates a huge space inside of which patience is required in almost daily doses.

The days I felt most peacefully patient were the days when I trusted the larger picture—when I trusted that the universe or God or some kind of wise higher power was in charge and not me. That kind of patience listened to the questions at hand, did what was needed for that day, and then turned over the rest to that greater wisdom. Things always did unfold in their own time; a patient acceptance allowed me to let go of pushing my own agenda and allowed me to settle in to the mystery of unfolding time.

*A patient acceptance of what is beyond my control will pave the way for me to honor each day's unfolding and not hurry into the next one.*

## *August 15*

***"You do not have to be good.
You do not have to walk on your knees
for a hundred miles through the desert repenting.
You only have to let the soft animal of your body
love what it loves."***

—Mary Oliver, *Wild Geese*

There is a writing exercise I use in classes I teach, and it begins with the simple phrase: "What I love . . . " It's an evocative phrase and an easy way to remind ourselves of the often-simple things we love and which energize and comfort us. My list would always include the color purple, my first cup of steaming coffee every morning in my fish mug, listening to certain beloved pieces of music. Given the day, there are many other items that might appear on this list.

To borrow from Mary Oliver, there is a soft animal inside each of us who knows what we love. Reaching for those loves in a healthy and daily way, and deeply appreciating those moments, is a beautiful way to stay energized. There are the moments where we might feel a need to prove our own worth—to prove our goodness, to prove our ability to walk across the desert. The wisdom of this poem reminds us to let go of the illusive need to prove ourselves by turning toward what we love and which nourishes us.

*As a caregiver, I do not need to prove myself in any way; I just need to bring what I love into the days of my caring.*

## August 16

***"We are best able to help others when we ourselves have learned the way to achieve serenity."***

*—The Twelve Steps and Traditions of AA*

Taking care of ourselves is a topic that comes around again and again for caregivers—because the needs are so great and because, for many of us, it sounds easier than it actually is. I often needed permission and sometimes needed to seek it from caring friends. Permission for what? Permission to make my own serenity a priority. I struggle with guilt, which all too often interfered with my seeking of serenity.

Caregiving challenged some long-held beliefs of mine. For much of my life, I brushed aside my own needs and truths. Compartmentalization coldly made compassion and self-care feel like they could not co-exist inside one relationship. Over and over again, I was given opportunities to learn how to deepen my own serenity and to see how that deepened my ability to be a compassionate caregiver.

*In the midst of the many pulls of our lives, we can know that every choice we make to enhance our spiritual serenity will nourish who we are as humans and caregivers.*

## *August 17*

**"A walk in nature walks the soul back home."**

—Mary Davis

Caregiving is soul work, and soul work has been defined as the bringing of the essential self (soul) out of hiding. Both our strengths and our weaknesses will be illumined on this trail. It is good and deep work, but it is not easy. Many days, it is hard to look at our flaws and perhaps also to see the flaws of our loved ones. Yet, we can honor that our days as a caregiver are illuminating deep aspects of our souls, or our essential selves.

On days when our soul is struggling with all that we are seeing and feeling, we can know that a solace is easily at hand. Even a short walk outdoors, in sunshine or moonlight, near oxygen-giving trees or near blossoming plants can restore our souls to a stronger sense of both sanity and serenity.

*When my soul feels fragmented, a walk in nature will always help my soul find its sense of home.*

## *August 18*

***"We are never more than one grateful thought away from peace of heart."***

—Brother David Stendal-Rast

Peace of heart can be hard to find on some days. It is hard to watch a parent whose memory or health is a pale shadow compared to what it used to be. Questions abound over the best way to deal with each crisis as it emerges. Worry is rampant, even though we all know it doesn't do anyone any good to worry. Yet, these wise words are helpful to remember on this journey, for often just a moment of gratitude can make peace seem possible again.

There are all the reasons why this is difficult, but if we look around, we can often find the consolations that exist. Perhaps our loved one is always soothed by a favorite TV show or piece of music or one helper who always cheers her up. Perhaps your loved one is especially grateful today for your care. We can focus on all the ways our loved one is in good hands and doing well, under the current conditions.

*Today's peace might be as simple as being grateful for my own health and for all the comforts available to my loved one.*

## *August 19*

***"To transform the suffering in our stories into a meaningful experience requires a courageous heart and a keen spiritual alertness."***

—Gail Straub

There is suffering in each one of our stories, and it is often particularly embedded in the caregiving and in the story of our loved one. Suffering includes but is not limited to physical and emotional pain, disappointment, grief, and loss of all kinds. Integrating suffering into our lives in a meaningful way is so important. As Straub states, this requires courage and an attuned sense of spirit.

There is always a lesson to be learned, there is always something to be gained from one's life experience. This can be missed when one is in too much of a hurry or if one gets lost in self-pity or resentment. The real lessons emerge as one faces each day with a spiritual courage—a desire to make meaning out of the ingredients of the day.

*Each day or experience as a caregiver can*
*provide me with meaning when I find*
*the courage to be open in this way.*

## *August 20*

***"The struggle of living in the moment, coping through stress of managing someone else's welfare through many unknowns, is what wears down even the strongest of caregivers over time."***

—Rev. Dr. Paul C. Hayes

The key two words of this quote are "over time." Most human beings are pretty good at jumping in for the short-term crisis, but most caregivers I know talk of the difficulty of a long, ongoing need where the end, or even the next day, is uncertain. So an absolutely common aspect of walking this trail is just plain feeling worn down. It happens to most of us.

And truly, the only—or at least the best—antidote is to take some time to do what rejuvenates us. For each of us, the way will be different. What is key is an activity that lets us relax, rest, and restore ourselves. Caregiving can be a long climb up a very narrow and demanding trail. Even those most in shape need some time to rest and slow down before picking up the pieces and walking on. Rested, we begin to again see the beauty of this trail. Exhausted, we miss that.

*When I am feeling worn down, it is a signal that I need to take a break and/or make arrangements for extra help. There are many ways to restore and rejuvenate myself.*

## *August 21*

***"But she was happier when we asked questions about the past, and happiest of all when it was clear we were listening, enjoying learning things about her that we hadn't known before and just glad she was there to tell us."***

—Jane Gross

Asking questions, listening, and just being there. Someone who has lived a long time has many stories inside of them. It is a true gift to be able to ask the right questions and then to listen closely enough to keep asking questions. The deeper gift is to respond to the story with laughter, interest, curiosity. So much lived life contained inside one body loves to come out, one story at a time.

It's an incredible opportunity to get to know things we, as the caregiver, may not have known or heard before. Choose a decade of your loved one's life—ask about specific events during that decade. Move on to another decade. Ask about jobs, old friends, activities . . .

*My interested and listening presence is all that is needed for my loved one to have the happiness of sharing him or herself today.*

## *August 22*

***"I learned that whatever we say means nothing, what anyone will remember is that we came."***

—Julia Kasdorf, "What I Learned From My Mother"

This meditation is an ode to showing up. Yes, sometimes what we say matters as well. But showing up is a key way of showing love, sharing love, and helping someone who is struggling to get through the day. As caregivers, we have made a commitment to show up. For some, this means daily. For others, it means several times a week. For yet others, it may mean weekly or something beyond that.

In the case of my mother, anticipation was half the pleasure. So if she knew ahead of time that someone was coming, that meant a lot to her. This worked at my end too; a scheduled visit gave me the knowledge that I would be showing up for her, but also to honor what we shared between us—as friends as well as mother and daughter.

*My choice to show up matters and will be remembered. It is part of how I carve out and create meaning in my life.*

## *August 23*

**"But caregiving takes a toll. There is often a huge cost to the caregiver and sometimes the care we give springs not from a well of love and altruism but from a bitter sea of resentful duty and obligation."**

—Henri Nouwen

The desire to care for others most often comes from a generous place in our hearts and souls. Yet, as humans, we can get so caught up in the needs of others that we extend ourselves beyond where we can safely go. Like an animal that has climbed too far out on a tree limb that is less and less able to support weight, we begin to feel un-centered, unsettled, on the verge of a fall.

When we find ourselves being easily irritated, cynical about our loved one or the world around us, or low on energy or desire, we are probably suffering from what has become known as "compassion fatigue." It is always possible to get back to a more compassionate center for caregiving, but the only route there is to give ourselves the needed attention and care that will rejuvenate us.

*When I find resentment or bitterness threading its way into my days, it is a sure sign I need to turn the light of compassion upon myself. This is how I move from bitterness to blessing.*

## *August 24*

***"Peace for my friends who sat quietly beside my bed during my long and mysterious illness, the comfort of their breathing enough. Peace for all our breathing."***

—Phoebe Hanson, *Peace for You*

Here are words of gratitude for the quiet loving presence of friends and family members when someone is not feeling well. Most of us, when going through a hard time, yearn for the companionship of a loved one who knows us and cares. At the very least, we yearn to have someone who checks up on us. Illness or physical limitations make all of us feel vulnerable, and often this is accompanied by feelings of loneliness.

These words, written by someone who received care at a critical time, remind us of the difference we make as caregivers. Our quiet presence, the comfort of sharing time and space and breath with our loved one, truly softens the hard edges of pain, loneliness, and uncertainty. There is a peacefulness that descends when our goal becomes simply to be with each other.

*Peace begins with me today as I show up for my loved one, sharing time and space in the way it is available to us today.*

## *August 25*

***"'Hope' is the thing with feathers***
***That perches in the soul,***
***And sings the tune without the words,***
***And never stops at all"***

—Emily Dickinson

In the face of unexpected losses, hope is a difficult thing to keep alive. Certainly, the COVID-19 has taken away many connections we previous took completely for granted: visiting and hugging loved ones; gathering for entertainment or music; coming together in communities for prayer, for condolences, or in celebration.

The quiet song inside, the tune that never stops, is about our human, ongoing need to keep loving and connecting with each other and finding creative ways to do so. Hope reminds us that what is most meaningful is never truly lost. It only changes form. All of the ripple effects of the pandemic create a global, collective reminder to take nothing for granted—especially the care we receive and give to the special people in our lives.

*Deep inside all of our spirits is a winged creature singing a song of hope. We can hear it through our windows, and our hearts, almost every morning.*

## *August 26*

***"As my mom's backup end-of-life caregiver, I know whereof I speak. The kindest thing she ever did for me was accept my help."***

—Carolyn Hax, advice columnist *Star Tribune*, April 6, 2020

The golden treasure and silver lining for most caregivers revolves around a deep knowing that it is a privilege to care for our loved ones. The river of caregiving is fed by many tributaries; proximity plays a role, time flexibility, emotional makeup, and more. An essential tributary to the process is the willingness of our loved ones to accept our help.

The reciprocity of kindness is key here. Many caregivers are perceived as kind, and we often are kind people who care. But the loved one who opens their hands and hearts to our help is also extending a kindness. This kindness is about sharing a difficult journey—a journey which is deeply human and deeply existential. It brings one face to face with the big questions in palpable ways. I, too, am forever grateful for the way my mother shared her journey with me.

*Today I will appreciate and cherish the full river of life that has immersed me in caregiving at this time. This privilege is truly a blessing.*

## *August 27*

***"Success is liking yourself, liking what you do, and liking how you do it."***

—Maya Angelou

Success is a difficult thing to quantify in many aspects of our world and is particularly hard to quantify in the world of caregiving. Yet, we probably attempt to judge ourselves through this lens, at least from time to time. Are we successful or not? Since outcomes are so often way beyond our control, we can't use outcomes as a measurement.

In fact, the only measurement that matters is how we feel about what we are doing. Sometimes the counterpoint may be how we would feel if we were not doing this caregiving. It takes a lot of courage and reflection to find ways to like ourselves and to like how we are as caregivers in this world. In fact, liking who we are as caregivers is integrally connected to liking ourselves. If an aspect of caregiving is not feeling right, if it engenders not liking ourselves, we can always find ways to change or adapt.

*A helpful guide for me along the way is to like who I am and to like how I am showing up.*

## *August 28*

**"Truths and roses have thorns around them."**

—Henry David Thoreau

There are moments of truth as we accompany a loved one through hard days of aging and/or failing health. Such moments of truth can be initially painful, as piercing as a thorn in one's finger. Moments of truth might include the x-ray that shows the broken bone which prescribes surgery for an already frail body. Or the moment when it becomes clear that one is no longer stable enough to walk without support or shower alone. Or when a new living situation or additional help needs to be found.

The pinprick is the new reality and, often, the work that lies ahead. The thorns of difficult challenges are definitely part of this path. But so too is the bloom of the rose, the help that can be found when one goes looking for it, the ability for medicine to ease pain and to enhance remaining strengths.

*The truth of the day's challenges is both thorny and full of potential for a new way of blossoming. Both are part of the fullness of the rose and of all that is real.*

## *August 29*

***"Forget your perfect offering***
***There is a crack in everything***
***That's how the light gets in."***

—Leonard Cohen

In our days as a caregiver, mistakes are made. We are only human, after all. We know how important clear communication is, but sometimes in the rush of a day we forget that; we accidentally leave someone out of the information chain. We forget an item our loved one requested. There are occasional cracks in anyone's organization plan. And you can count on there being cracks in our composure along the way.

Just as a crack in a wall lets the light in, so do cracks in our well-laid plans, unexpected fissures, let in light in a new and unexpected way. Most often, a crack will expose our own vulnerabilities. It is helpful to see this as an opening toward light, toward new awareness. For there is no perfect way to move through this time of caregiving.

*Today I will honor the cracks in my life and plans as a caregiver for how they let in the light.*

## *August 30*

**"Nobody has ever measured, even poets, how much a heart can hold."**

—Zelda Fitzgerald

The caregiver's heart is asked to hold a lot. Sometimes there are contradicting emotions that stretch our hearts hugely, and often the feelings are so intense. Then there are days that seem slow and tedious. I remember the day that the assisted living director told me my mother needed to move to a place where she could receive more care. My heart overflowed with tears as I stammered through thanking her for the four good years our mother had had in her facility.

We knew it had been coming, but the moment was still a difficult one. As I turned to share the news with my sister and then eventually with our other siblings, we felt daunted by the task and decisions facing us. Fortunately, we had done some research ahead, and we were able to spring into action and make the next needed decisions. But moving our 95-year-old mother into a new place, besides the work of any move, weighed heavily on our hearts. Yet, within a few days, we had her surrounded with beloved objects and people and wrapped in her familiar crocheted blanket.

*The ups and downs of this journey will stretch our hearts in many ways and, in doing so, will teach us of the immeasurable, bottomless love a heart can hold and express.*

## *August 31*

***"Love is not consolation. It is light."***

—Simone Weil

In a world spinning with changes—for instance, with the arrival of Covid-19 or the arrival of health issues in a loved one—there is often a sense that we can count on nothing. What felt like solid ground beneath us has become unsteady; our footing is off-balance and unsure. In times like this, I am always grateful for the way the sun rises every morning. Every evening, it exits beyond our view. But at times when we can count on little else, we can count on this amazing steadiness of how our planet moves in relationship with that most powerful star, the sun.

Difficult things always seem more doable in daylight. Fears are often diminished in the light of day. Love is like this steady light. And love illumines what the darkness hides. Love is a much stronger force than fear.

*Each day, we are awash in the steadiness of sunlight and the steadfastness of love.*

# September

## *September 1*

***"If you can, arrange for the physical environment at home or in the hospital (or other facility) to be as peaceful as possible. Place inspiring images in clear view . . . or a beautiful plant or flowers that remind one of nature."***

—Kirsten DeLeo

It is important for all of us to be surrounded by things that matter to us; this is especially crucial for those who are vulnerable. During the times our mother was hospitalized, often a single flower could cheer her up and bring the gift of both color and nature into the room. Over the years, we had to move her, and each time, the place didn't feel quite right to her until the pictures of her family had gone up on the table or wall near her. Small mementos and seasonal decorations often made her place more homey for her.

The loneliness of what she was experiencing could not ever be completely erased. Yet, those reminders on the wall of the full life she had lived, of all the people she had loved, of the holidays that had always provided meaning in her life, often brought her comfort and solace. For my father, the photograph on the wall of the farm he had grown up on and loved deeply was an important touchstone in the present that connected him to his past. These symbols and touchstones help a person feel at home in the present, despite the changes swirling around them.

*If I have already created a peaceful and meaningful setting for my loved one, then I will honor and make the most of it. I will also look around and see what other simple ways I can make my loved one feel calmer and more at home.*

## September 2

***"Getting sick when I was caregiving gave me a chance to rest and to remember how vulnerability both scares and opens a person."***

—Patricia Hoolihan, *journal*

Caregivers get sick. It happens. I remember being struck by a horrible cough when my mom was in assisted living. It was hard to stay away, but I didn't want to infect her. It gave me a good reason to rest more than usual. And on those first days, when I felt pretty miserable and compromised, my own vulnerability frightened me. What if I lost my strength? Or didn't get better? What then?

I did get better. The rest did me a world of good. I slowed down. I also got caught up on my teaching and other paperwork. The slowing down helped counterbalance a feeling that I was always behind. And, it reminded me of how vulnerable my mother must feel a great deal of the time, as she was often dealing with some pain in her body and a gradual loss of abilities. My own vulnerability helped deepen my sense of empathy for her. When I went back to caregiving her, when my cough finally subsided, I felt a renewed sense of compassion—and gratitude for my own health and ability to be there again for her.

*A few days of tending to our own health concerns has the potential for self-healing and reigniting the compassion we feel for the suffering of our loved one.*

## *September 3*

**"Feeding your father homemade oatmeal, scrambled eggs, and thickened drink becomes a spiritual act."**

—Caroline Johnson

There are opportunities along the caregiving journey for simple acts to become moments of reverence, for seemingly mundane action to transform into mysterious, sacred significance. Part of this is the slowing down and entering deeply into human frailty and vulnerability, entering even more deeply into the waters of love and care. In these moments, what could be felt as burden becomes an opening into a treasured moment.

Tenderness is not a quality I would have ever used to describe my relationship with my parents over most of my life. But there were many tender moments between us in their last years, months, and weeks. I still remember the cup of green tea I held to my father's lips on the day he died, the way he took in the warmth of that favorite drink of his. My mother's favorite treat weeks before she died was a caramel sundae. I would bring it to her. At first she fed herself, then I fed her small bites. When she closed her eyes and said, "Mmmm," I felt the air around us transform into a moment of radiant comfort. I still treat myself to caramel sundaes when I am missing my mother.

*Breaking bread together is a time-honored spiritual ritual in many cultures. I can honor that spiritual act today by sharing a favorite source of sustenance with my loved one and feeding our souls along the way.*

## *September 4*

***"And we are put on earth a little space,***
***That we may learn to bear the beams of love."***

—William Blake

These wonderful lines from one of our very wise poets speaks to the structural qualities of love. In any building, beams provide support, bear weight, keep a house standing, and hold a room together. All of that is also so true of beams of love. The idea that love is what we are here to learn in our relatively short stay on the planet is also an important message embedded in these beautiful words.

As caregivers, we provide support, we bear experiences that are emotionally heavy, we keep the family structure from falling down and apart, and we hold the love between ourselves and those we are caring for in a place of wholeness. We are on the arduous and often beautiful path of learning deep lessons of love in a very specific way—as a caregiver. As we learn to bear the beams of love, let us also find comfort and delight in what we are building.

*I can remind myself every day of all that I am learning about how to be a beam of love for the one I am caring for, and for myself. These lessons enrich me today and will enrich the rest of my life.*

## *September 5*

***"Always listen to your heart. The wisdom of your heart is the connection to your authentic power—the true home of your spirit."***

—Angie Karan

There were times on my caregiving path when I would feel strong emotions out of nowhere. Yet, at first that may not be obvious. At first, I might feel a tugging at my heart, an anxiousness in my breath, a faltering in my usually confident step. Or I might simply feel "off." All were signs of the impact on my heart and emotions of the intensity of the journey I was on.

It often took a flicker of recognition, a moment of reflection, an acceptance of and paying attention to what I was feeling. We caregivers tend to be sensitive souls. We are absorbing every day so much on this path that is full of human woundedness as well as cherished moments of joy. That is a lot for a heart to absorb, especially if we don't give it the light of our attention.

*When I feel something tugging at me, I can understand it is my heart speaking to me from its unattended darkness. Shine the light on me, it says!*

## September 6

***"I am part of the sun as my eye is part of me. That I am part of the earth my feet know perfectly and my blood is part of the sea . . . the mind . . . is only the glitter of the sun on the surfaces of the water."***

—D.H. Lawrence

It is all too easy to feel isolated and burdened as a caregiver. So often we are hurrying from one area of responsibility to another. Yet, we are part of a huge legacy called humanity, and our lives are interwoven with the vastness and tangibility of the natural world. We have a place in the universe and a place in our familial ancestry. We are accompanying those who are getting closer and closer to the edge of this particular gift of life on earth.

For caregivers, it is well worth pausing over to remember our place in a much larger picture—our place in our family lineage, and in the world around us. What beloved long-gone aunts, uncles, grandparents, great grandparents might be cheering us on? How might the growing things around us—tree leaves dancing in the breeze—be an integral and encouraging part of our journey?

*Today I will let the sun glittering on the water and the earth beneath my feet ground me in comfort and strengthen me. In often unseen ways, I am supported on this journey.*

## *September 7*

***"It takes grace***
***To remain kind***
***In cruel situations."***

—rupi kaur

Although an often necessary and natural part of life, both illness and aging can seem cruel. Loss can feel unkind and hard-edged. The diminishing of one's abilities almost always comes as a jagged shock. To face these parts of life with kindness and grace is at its core the challenge of caregiving. There are many definitions of grace, but among them are "courteous goodwill," "simple elegance." One of many potential synonyms is "tenderness." For many, grace is a spiritual blessing.

Sometimes we run into less-than-kind people caring for our loved one. How do we best advocate for them in these moments? It takes a gracefulness to know when to step in and when and how to speak up. But if we are coming from a place of tenderness towards our loved one and if we can exhibit courteous good will as we advocate, situations can be transformed in effective ways.

*Like all caring human beings, I have a spiritual reservoir of grace and strength which I can draw from when I need to face difficulties.*

## *September 8*

***"The root of suffering is resisting the certainty that no matter what the circumstances, uncertainty is all we truly have."***

—Pema Chodron

Caregiving could be likened to earning a black belt in the karate moves of uncertain times. One moment, we are donning the robes of an advocate and pushing for specific outcomes. In the blink of an eye, we are receiving news to which the only inevitable response is acceptance. Just as we are settling into a dance with recognizable moves, something changes.

We are always adapting to the changes, and they seem to come both slower and faster in the world of caregiving. As Pema Chodron, meditation and mindfulness mentor, reminds us, uncertainty is really an elemental part of all life. Some of our harder days as caregivers can most likely be traced to an old habit of wanting and expecting certainty.

*Today I can let go of my desire for certainty and embrace the deeper truth of uncertainty. Letting go gives me the flexibility and balance for the moves I need to make today.*

## *September 9*

***". . . even the most mundane and repetitive caregiving tasks can become a means for us to grow. With patience, with time, we can develop relationships of respect, listening, presence, and truthfulness with those we care for."***

—Henri Nouwen

Nouwen, a spiritual leader and author, writes beautifully about the opportunities to grow as a caregiving human being. He also writes of the importance of not ignoring our own needs as we do so. In fact, his wealth of experience and deep thinking shed light on the importance of listening to one's own needs in order to be a good caregiver.

In honoring our own needs, we become most readily available to listen, in the ways that really matter, to our loved one. It does take time and patience to find healthy and healing ways to be with our loved one. Time is on our side in this way, and patience always requires us to slow down.

*Part of being a caregiver requires honoring our own needs and then slowing down enough to truly listen and respectfully respond to the needs of our loved ones.*

# *September 10*

**"Sometimes we have to sift through the ashes to find a single spark."**

—Reb Dov Ber of Mezrich (Hassidic master)

My friend told me of visiting her mother who no longer remembers her, who had to be reminded she was her daughter. How very, very strange that is. Yet, a few moments into every visit, her mother would begin to relax. A sense of familiarity entered the conversation. She had a way of calming her mother that crossed the barriers of recognition—almost like an electrical current of connection pulsing beneath the memory loss.

There is no doubt that severe memory loss in a loved one upends everyone's sense of normal. Yet, a different way of relating does begin to emerge. One learns to rely on a quieter, more intuitive connection. Like finding quietly glowing embers in the aftermath of a hearth fire. Another friend told me that after the death of her mother, who hadn't recognized her in ten years, she still missed her "being," the physical presence of who she was, that longtime source of unconditional love.

*Even if there are only remnants of familiarity that remain, I can honor the glowing embers of this person I dearly love. I am grateful for her/his/their "being."*

## *September 11*

***"Crisis changes people and turns ordinary people into wise or more responsible ones."***

—Wilma P. Mankiller, Cherokee, 1987

One of the definitions of crisis is that it is a time of upheaval. One of the definitions of upheaval is the warping of part of the earth's crust. Upheaval is such a fitting word for certain aspects of caregiving. What has seemed solid beneath our feet, the earth's crust, our loved one's personality or intact mind, has been disturbed by unseen forces.

The crisis created by such upheaval requires ordinary people to stretch themselves into wiser and more compassionate beings than they have been. At a previous time, I could not have imagined bringing a cup of tea to my father's lips. At a previous time, I could not have envisioned how saying certain familiar prayers with my mother could calm her down. Their vulnerabilities created a space for me to creatively discover my own capacities for comfort and compassion.

*Today I will honor the extraordinary heart-opening moments that come my way.*

## *September 12*

***"At the edge of the mountain, a cloud hangs. And there my heart, my heart, my heart, hangs with it. At the edge of the mountain, a cloud trembles. And there my heart, my heart, my heart, trembles with it."***

—*Rain Song*, Tohono O'Odham, undated

Sometimes along the way, we find ourselves praying for a specific outcome. Please, please, please, we ask, usually for less suffering in one way or another. What I love about this quote is how it speaks to immersing one's heart in what hangs out there on the horizon, full of a mysterious potential. Hanging implies acceptance, while trembling implies a humbling realization of factors beyond one's control.

Sometimes we need to give ourselves over to the nameless horizon—whether it is rain or drought or snow or sunshine coming our way, we will, with trembling vulnerability, be ready to face it when it arrives. This wisdom lives deep inside of our hearts; we can trust our hearts. We can trust that the horizon will at some point move in and will focus the mysterious shroud of what we feel out there.

*What is out there on the edge of my awareness*
*will move in closer in due time.*
*I will be ready when it does.*

## *September 13*

**"The world is nothing but a school of love. Our relationships with our husband or wife, with our children and parents, with our friends and relatives are the university in which we are meant to learn what love and devotion truly are."**

—Swami Muktananda

I was stretching at the Y one morning and an idea entered me that is too late for me to try out, so I pass it on to you. From a young age, I was very close to my mother's mother, even in times when my mother and I were not getting along at all. Even then, I knew my mother appreciated the kindness and care I showed to her mother. So with her mother long gone and my mother in her last years, we sometimes shared recipes that had been her mother's.

My grandmother was a pie-maker. Neither my mom nor I took this up. But my daughter has. One of my grandmother's best pies, in my memory, is a peach pie. I wish I had often declared peach pie day when my Mom was still alive and brought fresh pie for us to share. It would have been fun and festive. It is hard to find the time to be creative when caregiving, so I offer you this idea. Have fun with your loved one—do it in a simple way. Connect the fun to a long-held family recipe or ritual. Love is a huge concept but can be easily connected to something as simple and delicious as peach pie.

*Today, or one day soon, I will let a simple and fun activity or outing shed light on the bond between my loved one and me. Something like peach pie can lift both of our spirits.*

## *September 14*

***"Sometimes asking for help is the most meaningful example of self-reliance."***

—Corey Booker, *Sometimes*

Many of us grow up with philosophies that encourage us to be strong and independent and hard-working. These skills are assets in many ways. In other ways, they work against us. No one can get through weeks or months of caregiving all alone without paying a huge price. When our stress levels are nearing a boiling point, often the only way to release steam is to seek support.

Support can be sought in many ways: is there someone you can ask to step in for you for a day, is there a specific task related to your loved one that you could ask another family member to take on, do you just need an understanding friend to bolster you, or is it time to seek additional professional help for your loved one? Self-reliance doesn't necessarily mean doing it all alone—it means that asking for help is part of keeping it all going in the best way possible.

*There are ways to release my caregiving stress, and asking for help is one of the most tangible. I will rely on that wisdom today.*

## *September 15*

***"Every encounter has within it the power of enchantment, if we're willing to look for it."***

—Richard Wagamese

True, enchantment might feel like a stretch in many caregiving situations. And yet, I have both experienced and heard many caregivers talk about those special, almost magical moments. One person discovers an object in her father's drawer, and when she asks him about it, he tells her of how it came to him fifty years earlier and why he has saved it all these years. Both are in tears by the end of the story.

A grandchild accompanies her mother, the caregiver. During their visit, she holds the hand of her grandmother who begins to talk about how much she loves them all and prays for them all. The granddaughter's heart is opened in this moment to the love and the force of the love flowing from her grandmother's words and hands. Tears are in her young eyes. In both cases, an almost out-of-time experience happened. Enchantment is a moment felt deeply within the hearts experiencing it.

*Enchantment opens up a larger sense of time; when such a gift arrives, I can fully honor and embrace it.*

## *September 16*

***"There are only four kinds of people in the world—those who have been caregivers, those who are currently caregivers, those who will be caregivers, and those who will need a caregiver."***

—Rosalynn Carter

This wise statement from former President Carter's wife reminds all of us of the many sides of the caregiving prism. It is multi-faceted. At some point in time, most of us will be in need of a caregiver; who knows where or when. And the rest of us have either already been a caregiver or we are immersed in it right now. If you are reading these words, you are probably in the thick of it. What you are learning today will inform those around you who will become caregivers in the years to come.

The prism of caregiving has many sides and dimensions to it. Prisms in windows catch the sunlight and cast dancing rainbows all around. Compassionate caregiving also catches sunlight and sends rays of color and light into the past, the present, and the future. Let my approach to caregiving catch light where I can and reflect it—for my loved one, for myself, and for all the potential and future caregivers around me.

*Roles change over time; let me honor my role as a caregiver today. Let me imagine this role as a prism catching and transforming the light of this day.*

## *September 17*

***"I guess, if you should ask, peace is no more than the underside of tired wings resting on the lake, while the heart in its feathers pounds softer and softer."***

—Mark Nepo

When I cast a backward glance at my years of intensive caregiving, I remember many feelings and experiences. But I am struck by how often, usually when driving back home after a visit, I felt tired. The busyness of all the demands of my life were a part of this. But also, the wear and tear of watching a loved one go through difficult days frayed at the edges of my energy.

Seeking peace means to honor that tiredness. I love the image of a bird resting its tired wings on the lake. Lakes speak to us of serenity and acceptance and silence. Walking by the lake near my home during those times always brought me solace—the solace of a quiet place to rest my tired wings and my beating heart. Sometimes just a half-hour walk helped to calm, soothe, and sometimes even rejuvenate me. It is hugely helpful to acknowledge and accept the tiredness that is part of this journey, rather than to fight it.

*When we feel the underside of our tired wings, we caregivers can seek the quiet spaces in our lives where we can find peace.*

## *September 18*

***"Love is the opening door***
***Love is what we came here for . . . "***

—Lyrics, *Love Song* by Lesley Duncan (sung by Elton John)

In the last few weeks of my father's life, as his health was going downhill quickly, I listened to the above song over and over again. My father, WWII veteran, a fierce father of eight children during long years of economic difficulty, was a man of song. In his last years, he appreciated any tenderness that came his way—through visits, simple time spent with his family, shared experiences.

As he neared his death, I was poignantly and powerfully reminded that love is what we all come here for, that caring for each other is ultimately the most important aspect of a life that is comprised of so many factors. Love is also what opens doors and crosses thresholds created by former hurts or grievances. As caregivers, we have a tremendous opportunity to remember and to enter the wise words of this song.

*If I can, I will listen to this song and let its beauty and its wise words carry me like a river current through the journey of this day.*

## *September 19*

***"The idea that nothing stays the same is central to Buddhism. Buddhists believe that loss and change are things to be accepted rather than causes of sadness."***

—powerstownnet.com

Certainly in the time of Covid-19, we have seen in an extreme way how quickly things can change and how dramatically. Yet even in more normal times, we see the inevitability of change at work. Human beings are endlessly creative and deeply in need of being connected to one another. The scenes of the Italians every night at a designated time making sustained noises of applause for the health care workers who are working so hard in the midst of such dire circumstances speak volumes. The need to connect. The gratitude for those who are on the front lines. The need to express that gratitude.

As caregivers, we can feel that larger sense of connection and gratitude. What happens in the larger sense, macrocosm, is mirrored in the equally important smaller sense, the microcosm. Caregiving is a practice in deep personal connection and gratitude, in a microcosm way.

*The changes coming my way are part of the universal reality that nothing stays the same. I can take deep breaths and work my way towards acceptance.*

## *September 20*

***"The ultimate lesson all of us have to learn is unconditional love, which includes not only others but ourselves as well."***

—Elisabeth Kubler-Ross

The ideal of unconditional love teaches us much along the way of letting go of expectations. It is not an easy lesson to live or embody. From the woman who spent decades of her life working with death and dying comes the wisdom of this simple statement. It is an ultimate challenge and lesson. The caregiving path is all about learning this lesson over and over again—to unconditionally love our loved one through difficult times and to love ourselves through the process.

When things go wrong, when we run into regret, when self-doubt hounds us, we get to keep returning to this challenge to love and accept ourselves as we are. When our loved one is crabby or obstinate, we get to keep returning to this challenge to love another through a difficult and charged time.

*I can appreciate caregiving for the daily opportunities it provides in often hard-earned lessons of love and self-love.*
*It is a gift which keeps on giving.*

## *September 21*

***"We don't have to do all of it alone. We were never meant to."***

—Brene Brown

When the road starts to feel lonely, it is a sure sign that we need to draw on our support systems. They can be found in many ways. If we are lucky, we have other family members who we can get support from, either emotionally or for help with caregiving tasks. If we are lucky, we have a supportive partner or good friends who understand what we are going through. Many places offer support groups for caregivers, and in those groups, there is a rich exchange of encouragement and understanding. Many of the people who are also involved in our loved one's care are part of an overall support team. Many community groups or churches provide support to caregivers.

As human beings, we are not hard-wired to get through life—let alone its struggles—alone. That is part of why our loved ones need us and why we also need them. Teamwork is really a beautiful thing and a heartwarming aspect of being human.

*Today I will be grateful for the many kinds of support which are helping me to stay sane and compassionate, even when I hit rough patches on this caregiving road.*

## *September 22*

***"Look closely and you will find that people are happy because they are grateful. The opposite of gratefulness is just taking everything for granted."***

—Brother David Stendal-Rast

One of the powerful ripple effects of COVID-19 is how it has reminded us of all the things in life we have taken for granted. Grocery shopping, although still allowed, is no longer to be done spontaneously or often. Instead, the mask needs to be found, a careful list made, the trips should be done efficiently and only as often as necessary. Yet, watching film footage of hundreds of cars waiting for food from the food shelf reminded me to be grateful for the ability to grocery shop at all.

Caregiving is another huge area so challenged by the virus and its lingering ripple effects. It has been heartbreaking to not be able to visit often, to hug our loved ones. Limitations make openings for creative and alternative ways of communicating. Cards, phone calls, waving from the window, having flowers delivered, using technology wherever possible are a few, but not all, of the options available. Ultimately, the essential need is to know we are loved. We can be grateful there are many ways to show and express our love as a caregiver.

*When I run into a limitation as a caregiver, I can gratefully turn to alternative ways to share love with my loved one.*

## *September 23*

***"Helping with the finances of an elderly loved one can provide peace of mind for everyone involved. Just be sure that you go about it the right way to avoid damaging your relationship."***

—Ben Luthi

Until the end of life and a bit beyond, finances are a necessary part of life. For many caregivers, helping with the finances of their loved one becomes part of the job at some point. Either through memory loss or the loss of other abilities, it just becomes harder and harder for the person to be in charge of their finances.

It is so important that this business aspect of life be dealt with in a way that is most of all respectful of your loved one, that is honest with all parties involved, and where the important information is shared among family caregivers. Lack of information can be very frustrating. Honesty and transparency are such important factors here and will go a long way to having finances be part of a relationship that is healthy and not damaging in any way to the loved one.

*I will honor the ways that financial obligations must be met and appreciate those who help with this.*

## *September 24*

**"Surprisingly, a simple beauty routine can help to reduce stress, anxiety, and depression."**

—Thebeautydeeplife.com

My mother's last trip to the hairdresser was a week before she died. And in fact, one of the phone calls I had to make after she passed was to cancel her next appointment. Getting her hair done was a source of pleasure for her right up to the end. So was a new sweater, often purchased for her by my sister. When I taught writing classes at her assisted living facility, one of the male writers would miss class only if he had to schedule his haircut at that time; it was very important to him. I was also often struck by the sweet volunteers who came to the facility to polish nails for the residents.

All of our lives, there is an exchange between how we feel on the inside and how we take care of and express ourselves on the outside. Sometimes one leads the other: the hair cut or shampoo, or the beautiful new sweater makes one feel better from the inside out. It's important as a caregiver to remember, honor, and make room for this.

*Small touches on the outside can help my*
*loved one and me feel better on the inside.*
*The message that moves deep inside*
*is that we matter and we are beautiful.*

## *September 25*

***"[Anthropologist] Malinowski suggested that people are more likely to turn to rituals when they face situations where the outcome is important and uncertain and beyond their control . . . "***

—Francesca Gino, Michael I. Norton on May 14, 2013 (*Scientific American*)

Family traditions and cultural and religious rituals become so important to someone who is aging or dealing with serious health problems. Even as a caregiver, I often felt the need to dial into a sense of a larger perspective. Rituals, because they span long stretches of time, speak to this timeless need and the need for a true connection.

All of our lives, my parents called each of their eight children and twenty-two grandchildren on their birthdays and sang Happy Birthday to them. In her waning years, it was important to help my mother make those phone calls and perhaps to sing along with her now more-frail voice. Engaging in this ritual she had practiced all of her life helped her to remember all the ways she had brightened her loved ones and reached out in love on their special days.

*I will honor the large and small rituals so important to my loved one. And I hope to carry them on into the future. Rituals, even ones we create, help honor the depth and passage of shared time.*

## September 26

**"It is not the load that breaks you down. It's the way you carry it."**

—Lena Horne, singer

The way we carry our emotions is often something that is felt in our bodies. Many professionals who do mind/body work suggest a few similar tips for helping our bodies deal with stress: making time to cry, any kind of exercise, hot baths and, if possible, massage or other body work. These are time-tested and tangible ways to help our bodies carry us through a time of stress. There is no doubt that caregiving is a path through uncertain woods; we carry a backpack full of concerns and plans and worries. We carry the canoe across the portage.

There are ways to lighten the load and to take some weight off our shoulders. We can share what we are carrying. Shedding tears lightens and cleanses us. Exercise always helps us to shed, let go, and free ourselves from unnecessary weight. Water in all forms has the magical ability to transform us; a hot bath can be particularly soothing. And if we can get healing hands to help soothe our tightened bones, that is an added bonus.

*Today I can pay attention to the ways my body is carrying tension and find ways to release it. I can find ways to carry my role more gracefully.*

## *September 27*

**"Care is a state in which something does matter; it is the source of human tenderness."**

—Rollo May, psychologist

Have you ever driven by a beach and seen those people with rods in their hands that are metal detectors? They walk slowly along the sand, moving their rod or wand—as I like to think of it—to find magic. The magnetic equipment helps them find silver, gold, and relics. Caregiving is filled with many vigilant moments, and often the magnetic magical moments come when we enter a shared tenderness with our loved one.

Tenderness comes in many forms: a shared moment of vulnerability, a moment of laughter, a moment of understood longing, an awareness of the gift of a shared life. It comes in moments when a surprise visit begets a tear, when praying together you enter a deep quiet space. It comes with the recognition of what you and your loved one are going through together.

*What we do every day as caregivers matters; this is most visible in the moments of shared tenderness. With my emotional metal detector, I will look for such a treasure today or soon.*

## *September 28*

***"When you recover or discover something that nourishes your soul and brings joy, care enough about yourself to make room for it in your life."***

—Jean Shinoda Bolen

In the busy life of a caregiver, it can be hard to grant permission to take care of ourselves. But doing so is very important. When I took the time to nourish myself, to remember the joyful things in my life, both my mood and my energy improved. There was a weekly exercise class I loved at that time, and when I fit it into my week, I emerged comforted and uplifted. Sometimes fitting in a walk around the lake near my home was exactly what I needed to remember the peace and joy of my life.

It is sometimes easier to see in others than in ourselves—the need for a break, the need to care for ourselves. But many of us have to set down the habit of guilt or the habit of working on the never quite done to-do list. Another way to honor self-care is to put it on the list. In a busy life full of demands, the moments spent in ways that nourish our souls will be like a pebble dropped in water—their ripple effects will travel in a beautiful way into the air and days around us.

*There are activities that nourish my soul and bring me joy; caring for myself by making time for them is part of what enhances my ability to give care to others.*

## *September 29*

***"The first act of love is always the giving of attention."***

—Dallas Willard

When a baby comes into this world, the baby needs to be fed and held and kept clean. All of those basic tasks require attention, tuning into the needs of a being who does not yet have language. The loved baby knows someone is attending to him or her.

In the same way, as adults in this world, we convey our care through the giving of our attention. As a caregiver, one of the most important gifts is the sharing of attention between us and our loved one: time shared, questions asked, stories listened to, needs responded to, food shared. There are many ways, but the basic ingredient is the giving of our full attention when we are with our loved one. That is both the practice and the gift.

*A simple and key part of this journey I am on includes giving my full attention when I am with my loved one or on the phone with my loved one.*

## *September 30*

***"So let us not grow weary in doing what is right, for we will reap at harvest time, if we do not give up."***

*—Galatians 6:9*

Often the seeds we plant during our time of caregiving are not always visible in the moment. Yes, we can see that our presence and care softens the hard edges for the person we are caring for, and that can be a rewarding in-the-moment experience, one to be gratefully received.

But there are other moments where one might wonder about the usefulness of this long and extended period of caring. There isn't a lot to show for it. At times, it can feel like the same problems keep surfacing and we are more tired as the days go by. There are definitely moments of discouragement along this journey. Hope is the seeded belief that we are doing the right thing. Right for us, right for this time and situation. What we are reaping is often still in seed form, awaiting the light and rain of time for it to blossom. We cannot always see what our time as caregivers is planting inside of us, but we can know that it is planted in a garden of love.

*Hope for today is believing that the seeds of love I am honoring in my role as a caregiver will bring a harvest I cannot yet quite see or imagine.*

# October

## *October 1*

***"Be here now. Be somewhere else later. Is that so hard?"***

—Ram Dass

Caregiving took me to some unusual places: assisted living, rehab facilities, doctor's offices, physical therapy, occupational therapy, a nursing home, hospital ERs, hospital rooms, tables surrounded by people older than I. Navigating different systems, different hierarchies, and unique personalities could be dizzying. If anything, it taught me to be flexible and how to be better at thinking on my feet. I still remember the kind and vibrant energy of many of the people who helped us with our mother.

A lot of humanity happens in all of these places. Vulnerability creates openings for compassion. The kindness of a particular physical therapist who encouraged and helped my mom get back to walking after a bad fall still reverberates inside of me. Her appreciation for my mother's courage helped me to see that courage more clearly myself. Over and over, I learned how much the kindness of anyone I ran into in all of those places touched me and my mother. Their actions warmed our hearts and our day.

*Wherever my caregiving journey takes me, if I fully enter the space of the here and now, there will be gifts and learning for me.*

## *October 2*

***"No water, no life. No blue, no green."***

—Sylvia Earle

With each of my elderly loved ones, there were times either near the end of their lives or during times of sickness when the ability for them to sip water was like a miracle. Something most of us take for granted—a normal part of everyday life. Yet, offering water to one who is reaching for it with all of their strength, whose body is putting effort into the taking of water into their mouth, into the swallowing, gives us pause. Into that pause comes the awareness of the simple healing blessing that hydration offers.

People can live for days on no other nutrition than water. And nothing signals the end more clearly than the inability or unwillingness to ingest water. So for this day, as a caregiver, let me celebrate where my loved one is on this journey and let me celebrate the simple gift and blessing of water. My mother was also a deep believer in the healing power of holy water, especially blessed. The sprinkling of that holy water always meant a great deal to her and inspired a sense of sacredness in the room.

*Today I am grateful for my ability to drink water, for my loved one's ability to drink water, and for the blessing all water holds.*

## *October 3*

***"Love is what you've been through with somebody."***

—James Thurber

My father and I had intense differences over the years. Yet, we kept mending things. And when his only remaining sibling out of 11 was about to go in for surgery at the age of 94, my parents and I were there to help and keep her company. I was very close to my Aunt Gert, and she was a beloved sister to him. Another cousin and I took turns keeping her company overnight in the hospital. At one point during this time, he turned to me and said in such a gentle voice, "Thank you for all your kindnesses to Gertie." Tears in my soul remain as I write the memory. He used her childhood name, not the name we called her by at the time.

The web of love wound around and through all these multiple connections. Perhaps our times of anger made us appreciate all the more our healing connections of love. Being in the trenches of caregiving, of sharing a path with a loved one that is difficult, provides many such moments. We are building a structure, an architectural feat, of love.

*I will deeply honor what I and my loved one are going through together. It is a structure with many rooms full of many different kinds of love.*

## *October 4*

***"Through her research and experience as a caregiver, Meyer found that many Vietnamese elders lack knowledge about Alzheimer's and wait a long time before seeking help or diagnosis. Sometimes, stigma drives them away from treatment . . . "***

—1/19/20 *Star Tribune* article written by Theodora Yu
about Oanh Meyer, researcher at UC Davis.

There are many cultural experiences and histories that impact the world of the sick or aging, and thus, their caregivers as well. In Meyer's research about the aging Vietnamese population, the impact of war trauma on aging is being studied. In immigrant populations, there can be a lack of understanding around medical care, especially available options.

Research and communication are key here. There are often more resources than one can imagine until you go looking. Asking questions of doctors and nurses and seeking out culturally specific support groups (many exist!) can be enormously helpful. The right information can make a huge and positive difference, but most of all, support groups provide the comfort of knowing you are not alone in trying to translate and live this challenging experience.

*There is a universal range of needs in the world of caregiving, and it is possible to find help that pertains to our own ethnicity, history, or religion. Such help and comfort is essential for me as a caregiver.*

## *October 5*

***"Learn to love the questions themselves like locked rooms and like books written in a very foreign language. Live the questions now. Perhaps you will then gradually, without noticing it, live along some distant day into the answer."***

—Rainier Maria Rilke

So many questions arise in the course of caregiving a loved one! Is this the right or best living situation for him or her? Is this the correct diagnosis and treatment? No situation is perfect, but what can I do to make this the best it can be? Who should I reach out to with my own questions? How do I keep myself centered and energized enough to do this job?

Each question is a path we travel down, asking and living as we go. The questions lead us, and many are answered—eventually. Entering fully into the questions is a huge part of this journey. Sometimes this entails reaching out to professionals or others helping us on this path, and sometimes it means quietly living the question as each day slowly reveals an answer.

*Today I will be at peace with all the questions inside me; the caregiver's journey is a path through the wilderness of so many unknowns. All I need to do is trust my next step.*

## *October 6*

***"Start by doing what's necessary; then do what's possible; and suddenly you are doing the impossible."***

—Francis of Assisi

Francis of Assisi, patron saint of Italy, known as lover of all animals and beings, lived in the 1200s. Think of how many centuries ago this was. These words of wisdom reach across time and seem to speak directly to the pilgrimage of caregiving. Make the first priority to take care of what is most necessary. What action needs to happen, what is the most obvious need at hand today?

It is always helpful to clarify what is the next needed step. The first step leads to the second step and then to a third. These words led Francis to sainthood, and although that is not the goal of caregiving, perhaps on some days, the goal is just making that next necessary step. What we can't imagine one day, we may find very doable as we keep moving one foot forward and then another.

*Today I will focus on the baby steps of necessity and trust that they will lead me on to all that is possible.*

## *October 7*

***"When we slow down, when we relax with our fear, we find sadness, which is calm and gentle. . . . Discovering fearlessness comes from working with the softness of the human heart."***

—Chogyam Trungpa

In the realm of caregiving, we will run into fears. Sometimes what is going on in our loved one incites fear. There can be fear around decisions that have to be made. Our own fears about how we are doing or holding up can also arise. From meditation master Trungpa comes the reminder to slow down when fear enters our body. Some of us feel it in our stomachs; many of us feel it in our breathing.

Fear is often a distraction, and very often it is a way of attempting to jump into an unknowable future. When we rest with our fear and breathe into it, often we will find beneath fear a sadness. Yes, there are sad threads to this journey, so many large and small losses. Sadness, when honored, can help calm and center us. Sadness, acknowledged to ourselves and perhaps to a few trusted others, opens our hearts.

*By honoring my fear and then the deep feelings beneath my fear, I will find the fearlessness I need right now as a caregiver—for my loved one and for myself.*

## *October 8*

***"The last of the human freedoms is to choose one's attitude in any given set of circumstances."***

—Victor Frankl

From the survivor of the concentration camps comes this incredible reminder about the power we have to choose our attitude. It is so easy to slip into the bad attitudes of self-pity or bitterness or cynicism. Often we are tired, and so these are easy defaults; after all, we are human. I know for a fact that I had days or moments of all of the above attitudes when I was actively caregiving. But they are not paths one wants to travel for too long.

I could have used more reminders about choosing my attitude. Transformation happens when one consciously wants it to. This doesn't mean it's easy to transform self-pity into acceptance, but it does mean it begins with both desire and intention. This is not an invitation to judge our difficult attitudes; it is an invitation to move toward an attitude that will ultimately feel better.

*No matter what the circumstances are that surround me today, I can choose an attitude of acceptance and hope.*

## *October 9*

***"Compassion is always, at its most authentic, about a shift from the cramped world of self-preoccupation into a more expansive place of fellowship, of true kinship."***

—Gregory Boyle

In the winter, in the northern state I live in, I cross-country ski. Out on the trail one day, crossing a frozen lake, I ran into an old friend. He was telling me that his partner was way ahead of him, and it had led him into a philosophical riff on how we ski alone, we often walk alone, we die alone. "But," I added, "we share the same trails." Exactly, he agreed.

Caregiving is about sharing the trail. One of us moves faster than the other, one of us moves more slowly in certain ways. We each have our own perspectives and awareness as we glide along. Some parts of the path are smooth, and some we lurch across awkwardly. The compassionate give and take of caregiving expands our awareness to include a wider view of the shared trail, the paths through daily life.

*Compassionate caregiving allows our hearts to expand, to honor the trail of life we share with many—and above all with our special loved ones.*

## *October 10*

***"No person can meet all the warranted needs of another, not even one's own children . . . "***

—Tove Pettersen

The glorious fall leaves remind me of how many factors go into creating their glory. Oxygen and air, warm summer sunshine. Rain has its impact, so does wind. So does the passage of time, the rhythms of day and night and of the seasons.

Time and again, I had to trust that there were many ways for my mother to find nurturing and comfort besides my company. I gave a lot, I gave what I could. But I also had to wrestle with walking out the door some days when she clearly wanted me to stay; I had another commitment or need of my own. I felt this to be a crucial challenge of caregiving—discerning when I needed to set a boundary and take care of myself. Realizing that I couldn't meet all those needs helped me. Realizing that there were others caring for her helped. Realizing that she had inner resources to draw upon: reading her prayers, watching a favorite TV show, picking up her phone. Sometimes just the passage of time helped her cross over a rough spot on the road.

*Realizing that I can't meet all the needs of my loved one, I will do what I can today and know that it is okay to also take care of myself. My loved one has other resources, more readily used when I am not available.*

## *October 11*

***"When people are vulnerable and hurt, silence takes on a much deeper meaning. These intimate moments of silence are like invisible threads that magically weave and hold together the truth of what really needs to be addressed."***

—Kirsten DeLeo

It is impossible to overestimate the importance of just being with someone who is going through a vulnerable time. Presence is truly the gift, and it is felt from both sides. Everything can be distilled at such times, down to an essence of who we are to each other. A friend describes her dementia-patient mother taking her hand and holding it in her own hands. Then her mother lifted my friend's hand inside of her own and held it to her heart. To the mother's heart. No words here. No need for a memory. Just a tender gesture of love and healing.

Hands over the heart—such a healing gesture. Hands held can quiet fears and stretch a warm band across loneliness. When my mom was sick, sometimes I would gently rub her forehead. She loved that. Sometimes I just sat beside her as she slept so when she woke up, she saw me there. This kind of caring silence provides a rare opportunity to slow down and rest deep inside of the beautiful web of relationship.

*I can learn to be comfortable with silence and, in fact, to allow it to carry me to deeper levels of awareness of this love journey.*

## October 12

**"Leave the door open for the unknown, the door into the dark. That's where the most important things come from, where you yourself came from and where you will go."**

—Rebecca Solnit

There are a lot of unknowns along the road of caregiving. Perhaps the biggest unknown is the overarching question: how long will this last? Most often, no miraculous recovery is at hand. For many of us, we know this journey for our loved one leads to their last breaths. There were many ups and downs for my mother, times we thought she was close to the end, and then she would "rally." It was exhausting, especially if I was attached to knowing what, where, when.

How and when a person will die is the biggest unknown. One can quietly prepare for it: it was helpful to talk with my Mom when she was open to it. About who she would like with her at the end, what songs she would like sung at her funeral, etc. Once she said she would like to take all of us, her eight children, with her. I smiled and said, "Yes, we know how you love us all. We will be with you in spirit."

*It is helpful to acknowledge and honor where this path leads, but to let go of specific timelines or expectations. The hands of the universe are wiser than our own.*

## *October 13*

***"A hot bath! How exquisite a vespertine pleasure, how luxurious, fervid and flagrant a consolation for the rigours, the austerities, the renunciations of the day."***

—Rose Macaulay

This British writer from the 1800s captures in a way that is both slightly amusing and also completely convincing the potential power of a hot bath. Perhaps this is a luxury we take more for granted in these modern days. Yet, it is worth listening to her simple wisdom. I especially love the description of the rigours and austerities and renunciations of the day. Included in the word austerity is the awareness of what is harsh and severe. Renunciation implies rejection.

In the course of some days of caregiving, we feel all of that: the rigor of what needs to be done, the harshness and severity of some situations, and the sense of rejection, of blocked paths along the way. The consolation for all of it? A hot bath. Think of it as a consolation, and a luxurious and exquisite one at that. Let that hot water and scent, if possible, wash over you and comfort you as deeply as you need it. Let it in. All the way in.

*When my day is done, or soon, I will treat myself to the consoling comfort of a hot bath. I will let it assuage any deep pain I am carrying today.*

## *October 14*

***"The earth laughs in flowers."***

—Ralph Waldo Emerson

Laughter can be described as the sound of merriment or joy. There is nothing merrier or more joyful than flowers, which grow in such a stunning variety of colors, shapes, and sizes and emerge during different times of the year. The variety of flowers that grow on this planet is beyond amazing. Sunflowers, daffodils, hyacinth, azaleas, to name a few; entire books would be needed to catalogue them all.

When we need to lighten our hearts or the heart of our loved one, we need only look around at the flowers available to us. The lilac plucked from a neighbor's tree always brought my mother great joy and does so still for me today. Flowers are not only a lighthearted reminder of joy, they are also tenacious. Think of the purple blossom that finds its way through a crack in a sidewalk or a granite ledge in the wilderness.

*When I am in need of laughter, I can look for a flower to cheer me up—that there are so many to choose from reminds me of the abundance in this world.*

## *October 15*

***"The secret of health for both mind and body is not to mourn for the past, nor to worry about the future, but to live the present moment wisely and earnestly."***

—Buddha

This is much harder to do than it sounds. Of course, a loved one who is "failing to thrive" is both anxious about what is ahead and sad about losing strengths and abilities they used to have. And you, who are in the trenches with them, feel these same concerns. Still, it is always a good reminder that the things that cannot be changed are in the past and that the future is a mysterious blank slate.

So why not bring your focus and their focus into this particular day—this day with its simple comforts, whatever they may be. A focus on the day's gifts might include a favorite aide on duty, your time with each other over a cup of tea or coffee, a phone call that comes in from a grandchild, or rereading a card that recently arrived in the mail. Perhaps there is a funny story from your life to be told and appreciated.

*When I am with my loved one, help me remember to enjoy that moment and stay inside of it and to deeply appreciate its small gifts.*

## *October 16*

***"Today may there be peace within. May you trust that you are exactly where you are meant to be."***

—St. Teresa of Avila

Restlessness and self-doubt can find their way into the cracks of any life, but perhaps especially a life that is demanding in its daily tasks and in its witnessing of a loved one's shrinking abilities. Trusting the "rightness" of the path of caregiving is so important. Trust becomes the river we swim in, and if we believe in the river we are swimming in, we will feel more at peace. We will be traveling with the current rather than against it.

From this Spanish saint in the 1500s come words of wisdom across time and space. Like many before us, we can enter the challenges of the day knowing that we are meant to be here, today, caring for our loved one. Whatever problems that arise this day can be faced, and a solution can be found. Since we are exactly where we are meant to be, that means we have all the resources available within us or near us.

*Peace is possible within me today; I need only trust, as many have before me, that I am exactly where I am meant to be, that the current of life is carrying me.*

## *October 17*

***"The greatest compliment that was ever paid me was when one asked me what I thought, and attended to my answer."***

—Henry David Thoreau

Hundreds of years ago, Thoreau carved out a distinctive path for himself by paying attention to the natural world and making that the center of his life and of his writing. From this deeply sensitive sage comes the reminder of how important it is to be sought out and listened to. In spite of all Thoreau's accomplishments, what is memorable is what it meant to him to have someone ask him what he thought—and then listen.

This is so deceptively simple and profound. It is a beautiful reminder for us caregivers to take the time to ask our loved ones what they are thinking and then to truly pay attention to and tend to their answer. This only takes time and some conscious effort. More than once I have heard someone wistfully say, "I wish I had asked my father about that when he was alive or when he had his memory."

*Thoreau's words are an important reminder to me to ask my loved one what he or she is thinking and then to truly listen and attend to what is spoken.*

## *October 18*

***"At the deepest level, there is no giver, no gift, and no recipient . . . only the universe rearranging itself."***

—Jon Kabat-Zinn

There are moments in caregiving when one fully realizes that the exchange between yourself and the person you are caring for is one where help and need are melted into the much larger crucible of mutual care. This concept of the universe rearranging itself is truly what has happened. Roles have shifted and changed over time. Yes, there is a dance between need and ability. But across long stretches of time, most of us are going to walk through a wide range of human experience.

The universe has currently rearranged itself so that we caregivers are inside the giving part of the dance. Yet, there are multiple opportunities to feel at deep levels the overriding truth that what is given and received melds together. When this happens, we can know that deep waters are carrying us along on their current.

*Today I will let the deep current carry me;*
*beyond giving and receiving we are, together,*
*part of a universal flow of life and living.*

## *October 19*

***"This is a wonderful day. I've never seen this one before."***

—Maya Angelo

On any life journey, it is good to pause and appreciate the gift of life, of breath, of each day. Such a pause invites us into a deeper awareness of the precious gift of life itself. It is all too easy to waken, to hurriedly enter the day's demands, and to hurriedly move through that endless to-do list. Yet, even a brief moment of awareness can imbue all of our actions with the added light and colors of gratitude.

As caregivers, our sense of burden and responsibility can be lightened by allowing in the illumination of gratitude. Letting in the light of grateful appreciation doesn't take long; it just takes a conscious effort. It takes remembering to do so. This allows us to open our hearts to the furtherings of each day, whatever shape and form they may take.

*I am grateful for awakening today and for all the gifts of this day—the hard ones and the easy ones.*

## *October 20*

**"Nature itself is the best physician."**

—Hippocrates

Nature comes to us and can be sought in both large and simple ways. When my loved ones were more and more homebound, sometimes the sight of a bird out the window could provide a special moment. Angles of sunlight, the beauty of a snowfall, and the way wind danced with branches out the window were all ways that nature entered our hearts, despite being more confined to indoors. Flowers and plants also bring the healing quality of nature inside; the aroma and color of any bloom provide pleasure.

Often, as I left my parents' place, or my mother's assisted living facility, the fresh air revived me. Whatever treats the day's weather had for me, I fully absorbed. Sunlight, starlight, even patterns of clouds moving across the sky provided healing moments, and I hungrily yearned for them. Long goodbyes are rugged; nature provides a daily solace and opportunity for healing and acceptance.

*Today I will let nature, in its myriad forms, enter and heal my day, and I will look for ways to provide the same opportunity for my loved one.*

## *October 21*

***"You are imperfect, you are wired for struggle, but you are worthy of love and belonging."***

—Brene Brown

These words come from the bestselling author and researcher on how humans live with courage and vulnerability. She states that we are wired for struggle and that all of us are imperfect. These two facts may at times seem obvious, but it is helpful to be reminded of our shared humanity. Paired with this knowing is a reminder that every one of us is worthy of belonging and loving ourselves and feeling loved by others. Her words are both powerful and highly read: this speaks to the deep need among so many of us for her message.

As caregivers, we definitely experience struggles and our own imperfections. We probably run into both almost daily. So the needed reminder is that we are worthy of love and belonging as we struggle along. We can seek out love, we can grant ourselves small daily acts of self-love and self-acceptance. We can know and settle into the places where we feel we belong.

*Belonging and love go together. I belong on this path as a caregiver; that is why I can find ways to love myself and my loved one every day.*

## *October 22*

***"You prepare yourself for one sorrow***
***but another comes.***
***It is not like the weather,***
***You cannot brace yourself,***
***The unreadiness is all . . . "***

—Derek Walcott

Often in the world of caregiving, there are hard moments of loss. Some kind of loss has invited us to enter this path through life for a time. Few of us feel ready for it at the beginning. And few of us feel ready for the changes and surprises we encounter along the way. That is part of why caregiving opens our hearts so much. Since there is no way to be ready for all it entails, the surprises have a lot to teach us. Over and over again, we are asked to let go of preconceived ideas and notions about ourselves and the ones for whom we are caring. We are asked to let go of knowing what is ahead.

Bracing ourselves implies tightening up and shielding ourselves. Rather, taking off the armor is a much more heartwarming experience. The more we can accept and embrace a state of unreadiness, of openness to whatever is ahead, the better equipped we are to fully enter into the experience.

*There is no weather forecast to tell me what is ahead; rather than bracing myself, I believe I will handle whatever comes in the best way I possibly can.*

## *October 23*

***"All day it continues, each kindness reaching toward another—a stranger singing to no one as I pass on the path, trees offering their blossoms . . . "***

—Dorianne Laux, *For the Sake of Strangers*

Kindness matters. I remember simple acts of kindness that touched me when I was in the trenches as a caregiver. A neighbor brought us dinner one night. A sibling sent me a thank you card. A yoga teacher told me I moved wisely in my body, which reduced me to tears on a day when I felt anything but wise. It's a good reminder to all of us; people who are going through hardship are particularly open to and in need of kindness.

Sometimes kindness comes in the form of the natural world offering its gifts to us. Sometimes it comes unexpectedly from complete strangers. Sometimes we exchange it with the people we know and love the best.

*Let me be open today to kindness in all its possible forms, and let me remember to pass it on.*

## *October 24*

***"Is dit an mac an saol, we say in Irish—'life is very strange.'"***

—Padraig O'Tuama

As caregivers, we are always part of a much larger community. Things happen that are beyond our control. There were times when my mother's assisted living facility was shut down due to a contagious flu outbreak. Certainly in the days of the COVID-19 outbreak, we see how impacted our loved ones are, how impacted and limited are our forms of caregiving.

A scene that was often replayed on news broadcasts, during the early days of COVID-19, was of a young woman outside her grandfather's window, showing him her engagement ring. They were separated by the safety of thick glass, but everyone who saw this felt the shared love. We also felt the difficulty of the necessary barrier. How strange we might have found the scene just a month before; how much sense it makes in the new strangeness of life. Extenuating circumstances affect us all, but we can always find alternative ways to express and share love. There are endless possibilities.

*When circumstances beyond my control create barriers for the usual forms of caregiving, I can be inventive. I can show up outside a window, call, email, Face Time, and/or send a card. All are forms of love.*

## *October 25*

***"Success is the sum of small efforts, repeated day in and day out."***

—Robert Collier

So often we wonder if we are doing the right thing as caregivers. I often wondered, am I asking the right questions? Am I showing up in the most authentic way? Am I trying to do too much or too little? It is hard to feel successful as a caregiver because the needs are often so ongoing, ever-changing, and bottomless.

The above quote is a beautiful reminder that all of our small efforts contribute to a successful path of lightening and brightening the load for our loved one. Each small effort, though it may not look or feel like much, matters. It's an impossible role to quantify—caregiving. It continually invites us into a larger perspective; today's efforts to express and exchange love are part of a much larger web of love. This is truly success.

*My sense of success as a caregiver requires that I believe in the many small efforts on my part and on the part of those around me.*

## *October 26*

***"When one tugs at a single thing in nature, he finds it attached to the rest of the world."***

—John Muir

I always return to birds. What is it about birds? When walking with my two-year-old granddaughter, she would stop dead in her tracks at the sight of a robin. "Boid, boid," she would say, pointing in excitement. She reminds me that even a simple robin is a miraculous sighting. The robin will hop, dig for worms, fly away, and above all, sing.

Singing birds always lift my spirits. They lifted my mother's spirits too. More than once, when out for a walk with her in the wheelchair, we would pause to watch and then listen to the singing of a bird. Both the 90-something loved one and the two-year-old loved one reminded a grateful me to pay attention to the birds around me, to let their singing enter my heart.

*Sharing nature, even in simple ways, helps inform the love we have for each other through the many-layered and multiple loves of the natural world. We are all connected.*

## *October 27*

***"I believe in the sun even when it is not shining . . . "***

—Unknown, poem written by Jewish prisoner in Nazi concentration camp

Most of us who are caregiving have a lot to be grateful for and also carry a lot of responsibility at the same time. It is important to be honest with ourselves about both. I have heard the above words both sung and recited, and they always move me. Even in a most dark time in our collective history, those who faced unbelievable darkness of humanity found ways to believe in the possibility of light.

That example shines through the decades and reminds us that no matter the difficulty of a dark day, we can believe in the possibility of finding our way through it. Even on days when no questions get answered and we see suffering around us, we can believe and know a better moment will arrive. We can believe the sun is there warming us and lighting the way, though we can't yet see it.

*Hope is a thread I can choose to hang onto; part of how I do so is blind belief, and another part is gratitude for what is at hand.*

## *October 28*

***"It is good to have an end to journey towards; but it is the journey that matters in the end."***

—Ursula LeGuin

The gift of caregiving is that it often forces us to slow down and to focus on each day, a day at a time. There is not usually an ambitious goal other than to help our loved one either return to health or gracefully move through their health challenges. Therefore, the end goal fades into the distant future, but the journey of today, of this week, is right before us.

The way we journey through these seemingly simple and often repetitious days is really what matters. Are we being kind to ourselves, are we being compassionate to our loved ones, are we being appreciative of those who are supporting and helping us? It's a creative journey; we can keep finding ways to brighten each day—for ourselves and for our loved ones.

*As I focus on the journey at hand, let me do so with access to simple joys and appreciation.*

## *October 29*

***"My imperfections and failures are as much a blessing from God as my successes and my talents, and I lay them both at His feet."***

—Mahatma Gandhi

Whether or not we believe in a God or a male God, we can borrow and learn from the wisdom of this wise and peace-loving leader, Gandhi. So often, many of us are hard on ourselves. When our vulnerabilities or weak points are revealed, we fall into self-criticism or even trying to hide our faults. To see them as blessings can be quite revolutionary. And perhaps great people are great in part because they have learned to embrace their darker sides.

Our vulnerabilities are our connection to the rest of humanity. When I felt inadequate to the day's demands, if I opened up to the right person, a recognition flowed between us. That recognition was often the blessing of the day. When I saw myself as falling short as a caregiver, that shortcoming often led me to the help I needed to make the next step. The next step was often about what my loved one needed or what I needed in order to remember I was worthy of love too.

*My imperfections and my talents are blessings*
*I can be thankful for—they make me*
*the unique human being that I am.*

## *October 30*

***"Being deeply loved by someone gives you strength, while loving someone deeply gives you courage."***

—Laozi

A definite aspect of being a caregiver is needing to advocate, often in a variety of settings, for the well-being of our loved one. This can mean asking tough questions of medical personnel, following up on the kind of care we want our loved one to receive, or asking for more or different kinds of help.

Advocating requires both clarity and courage. First of all, clarity: paying attention, doing some research, asking questions. Then the courage to speak up: this is fueled by the love we have for the one we are caregiving. We can exercise our personal strength, which perhaps in many ways was encouraged by our loved one, to find the courage to say what needs to be said and to make the changes that will be best for our loved one.

*Strength and courage, from a deep source of shared love, are part of the fuel for the necessary moments of advocating along this road.*

# *October 31*

***"Every particle of creation sings its own song of what is and what is not. Hearing what is can make you wise; hearing what is not can drive you mad."***

—Sufi poet Ghalib

From this Indian poet of the 19th century comes a beautifully rendered reminder to keep the focus on what is, not on what isn't. Our loved one is no longer able to walk far on her own, but her thoughtful inquiries into all family members and her joy at their achievements are a reminder to slow down and take in what is happening around us.

Wishing for what isn't is something we all fall into; the trick is not to stay there. The challenge is to keep returning to the songs of life that are singing to us right now. There is a wisdom that comes when we listen to what is reverberating inside of even small, seemingly mundane moments.

*As I listen to the song of what is happening*
*for me and with my loved one,*
*I will let its music infuse my day.*
*Wisdom often comes from quiet whispers.*

# November

## *November 1*

***"Walk in nature and feel the healing power of the trees."***

—Anthony William

Healing! As human beings, we seek healing during many phases of our lives, if not every day. This desire, longing, and yearning for more wholeness, for a gathering of the splintered edges of experience, is especially tangible for caregivers. The edges of fatigue, of sadness, and of frustrations often made me feel like every nerve ending was jangled or jagged.

No matter where we live, we are surrounded by trees, and they are nature's beneficent gift to us. I have a favorite row of willow trees which always makes me feel comforted and reminds me of the power of grace as the trees' wispy branches sway in the wind. In the summer time, the scent of pine needles can refresh me in the time it takes to draw a couple of deep breaths. When we tune in to the power and beauty of the trees around us, a simple walk will provide healing.

*The trees that surround me are there for me to turn to when I am in need of the deep healing that nature provides.*

## *November 2*

***"[Mature care requires] an ongoing reflection on how one interacts with others, how well one understands and responds to them, as well as how one cares about oneself."***

—Tove Pettersen

One of the most difficult aspects of caregiving is taking care of oneself. The external needs always seem much more pressing. And many of us have an inclination to take care of others first. All too often, that tricky element called guilt plays at the edges of everything. We feel guilty about drawing lines in the sand, about taking care of our own needs.

And yet, self-care is essential to being a caring caregiver. When we begin to feel over-burdened, easily irritated, or downtrodden, these are signs that we need to carve out some time and ways to feed our own needs. Perhaps it's a need for exercise, fresh air, a night of music, time with a friend, time to read, or time to slow down. Part of a day, a full day—even small things can make a difference. And best of all is to build taking care of yourself into a regular schedule, to take care of yourself before you feel too downtrodden.

*An essential part of being a caregiver is reflecting upon my own needs and understanding that I need to care for myself, as well as my loved one, in order to be the kind of caregiver I want to be.*

## *November 3*

***"I once asked a bird, 'How is it that you fly in this gravity of darkness?' She responded, 'Love lifts me.'"***

—Hafiz

I find among fellow caregivers an understanding of the forces of gravity at work in caregiving. There is the weight of the many pulls we feel, the weight of the seriousness of what we are looking at and facing with our loved one. There is the weight of the endless to-do list. There is the weight of the responsibility of caring for someone who is going through a very difficult process.

As Hafiz's bird reminds us, wings can be lifted into flight in spite of gravity. The force lifting the wings of any caregiver is that of love. This love lifts us out of the darkness we feel from time to time. Bluebirds, robins, cardinals, and many more birds are all around us, reminding us that we can lift ourselves into the music of flight and light in spite of the forces of gravity all around us.

*Look deep into the eyes of your loved one or your own eyes and you will find the love and light to lift today's burdens into wings of kindness and care.*

## *November 4*

**"When you do something noble and beautiful and nobody noticed, do not be sad. For the sun every morning is a beautiful spectacle and yet most of the audience still sleeps."**

—John Lennon

When one hears the role of caregiver talked about, the word "thankless" often comes up. Many of us don't feel appreciated for the many things we do, many of which are hard to see for those who are looking from a distance. It is not like we expect to be thanked for everything, but likely much of what we do is behind the scenes, small gestures invisible to many. The phone calls to doctors, arrangements for medications, details about food, and small ways to brighten up a day. It all takes time and thoughtfulness.

Yet, when we are feeling unappreciated, it is helpful to think of how the sun rises every morning and often without applause. It shines its glorious light on those who are oblivious as much as on those who are paying attention and gratefully absorbing sunrise. This image is helpful to keep in mind. We do what we do because, like the rising sun, it's who we are. Moments of thanks are wonderful, but not essential.

*Today I will know that even if all my efforts are not noticed, they provide a steadfast light that matters in this world.*

## *November 5*

***" Our heart is our ultimate source of power."***

—Lily Collins

Caregiving is above all a journey of the heart. But it is so easy to get caught up in all the busy needs of caregiving and of the rest of our lives that we forget to pay attention to what our hearts are carrying. When something is tugging at us, when we feel uncommonly distracted, this might be just the time that we most need to tune in and listen.

Is our heart burdened by sadness and grief? Do we need to take action to soften the aloneness we are currently feeling? Is there a conversation we need to have with our loved one that has been weighing on us? When we open our hearts and listen, then our hearts—which feed our intuition—can lead us to the next important doorway. A simple acknowledgement of our own deep feelings can surprise us with its ability to heal and transform us.

*Today I will tune in and listen to what my heart most needs and wants—this is how I also take care of my loved one's heart.*

## *November 6*

***"Do what you can, with what you have, where you are."***

—Theodore Roosevelt

Over a hundred years after his presidency, these wise words still resonate. They particularly resonate during times when we face obstacles and situations that cannot be changed. Obstacles come in many forms; COVID-19 is one that very few saw coming. Its ramifications rippled and are still rippling, turning lives upside down and inside out in a matter of days. The need to adjust has been and will probably continue to be breathtaking in its sweep and speed.

The challenge to caregiving in such times is palpable. We can only do what we can: reach out in safe ways, honor the codes of safety for the protection of our loved ones. We can also believe in our loved ones; they each have inner resources they can rely on and deepen into during times of duress. Creativity and acceptance can work together when we run into obstacles as a loved one and as a caregiver.

*Let me be creative about the ways I can reach out in difficult moments, and let me accept and find peace inside the limits of where I am and what is available to me.*

## *November 7*

***"Compassion brings us to a stop, and for a moment we rise above ourselves."***

—Mason Cooley

There were moments in the long journey with my mother when time literally stood still. A moment of awareness crept in; a moment of tenderness touched me; a realization of how precious and limited was her time left on this earth. Compassion and connection lifted such moments. Here was this woman who had given birth to me and always loved me. We had spent years misunderstanding each other. As her strength waned and her end drew near, we were companions. Two women growing older, together.

Beyond all the complexities of a parent/child relationship, we were two people grappling with what it means when one nears the end. The Great Mystery, as we sometimes called it. She was so close to it. I felt close to it when I was with her. I was with her in her final moments, a gift I will treasure every day of my life. Being her caregiver, her companion on her journey as much as I could be, truly slowed and deepened my world and my own sense of this great shared mystery.

*Today I will treasure the abundant gifts of compassion that are all around me on this caregiving path.*

## *November 8*

***"A caring heart that listens is often more valued than an intelligent mind that talks."***

—Michael Josephson

My friend's father, who lives in a memory care unit, can really get going with telling stories and talking to imaginary people. What my friend has learned to do is to enter into the story, ask questions, and respond. My friend has learned it does no good to try to rationally set the record straight, unless it is necessary as a way to protect his father's personal safety. Instead, he listens. And into the story comes familiar fragments, wildly and imaginatively reconstructed.

With a caring heart, he hears the humanity embedded in the story. He enters the story and often comes away with a new awareness about his father. Whether the person we are giving care to suffers from memory loss, emotional instability, or physical problems, we can bring our listening ears and caring hearts to the story they want to tell today.

*Today, my listening ear and caring heart can enter the room together.*

## *November 9*

***"How I Would Paint the Leap of Faith: A black cat jumping up three feet to reach a three-inch shelf."***

—Lisel Mueller, *Imaginary Paintings*

I vividly remember moments where I wondered how we would solve the next problem for our mother or father or our elderly aunts and uncle. Medicines needed to be changed in some way or form, or we ran into the need for further tests or treatments. Sometimes a change in living arrangements had to be researched and organized. Crises had us scrambling.

I love this image of the cat, believing in its own power to leap. If you have ever watched a cat about to leap, it eyes the distance, observes, almost looks like he/she/they is calculating, and then: leaps! We, too, can carefully eye what is in front of us, ponder, observe the options closely, and then let the belief that we will figure things out impel us forward.

*I can allow this somewhat humorous image of the leaping cat to inspire my own leap of faith; I and my caregiving team will figure out the next needed step.*

## *November 10*

**"As flickering candles burn and pierce the darkness, we thank you, for the light that illumines our soul and gives us breath."**

—Teri Larson, *Evening Thanksgiving*

This line from a Vespers prayer is a wonderful invitation into gratitude at the end of the day. This practice of reviewing a day and noticing what one is grateful for is encouraged by many spiritual directors, meditators, and mindfulness mentors. Candles are optional, although their simple flames often help provide a sense of sacredness. We can begin with being grateful for "the light" from any source which illumines our soul and for the simple and elemental gift of breath.

As caregivers, it is helpful to remind our tired selves at day's end to pause for a moment of reflection, of feeling grateful for the gestures of care we have given and received this day. We might also reflect on what we would do differently tomorrow. But the more important thing is to pause and remember to appreciate our own breath, the light the day has shed on our souls, and the breath we share with our loved one.

*Let me take time at day's end to be grateful for the gifts of each day.*

## *November 11*

***"May you use the gifts that you have received and pass on the love that has been given to you."***

—St. Teresa of Avila

Somehow, for each of us, our gifts have led us to this role as caregiver. It may seem like happenstance more than anything —here is our beloved spouse or parent or sibling or other relative or friend in need, and we are in a position to help with their care. But it also elicits our gifts—of kindness, of compassion, and more. There is also the gift of mental acuity: we see many needs and find a way to meet them.

Above all, these gifts are conduits for love. The love we have known and received in our lifetime has prepared us to express love in this difficult time. Nothing is more important or elemental to the human spirit, nor to a sense of meaning in our lives. Whether it's our listening ear, our ability to advocate, or our thoughtfulness to show up with a cheerful decoration, these gifts matter.

*Our gifts may seem small, but they are important conveyors of love.*

## November 12

**"It did not really matter what we expected from life, but rather what life expected from us."**

—Victor Frankl

Okay, I admit that there were days when I was a caregiver that I wanted to whine about some aspect of it—usually about feeling frustrated, tired, or pulled in too many directions. Sometimes I felt like the days produced little of what I might have dreamed of or expected of life. There were days when sadness ruled, when I felt the loss of other ways of being inside of my day.

And yet, it was and is helpful to remember these words from someone who survived a concentration camp. Many before us have spent days in unexpected and less than ideal ways—and many in ways much harsher than we can truly imagine. It is helpful to consider not what we expect but rather what life expects from us. In this way, we can step more fully into embracing this life and rising to what life itself, in its expanded sense, expects of us at this time and inside of this role.

*At this moment, life expects me to be the best caregiver I can be; I can rise to do so with the best of what I have to offer.*

## *November 13*

***"Television is becoming a collage; there are so many channels that you move through them making a collage yourself. In that sense, everyone sees something a bit different."***

—David Hockney

The father of a good friend of mine had a quick and unexpected move into a nursing home. It was very difficult for him. One of his favorite weekly TV shows was Sixty Minutes on Sunday evening. They moved him in on a Saturday. By Sunday afternoon, the most important person in the family became the one who could hook up the TV in his new room.

With beds made, coffee pot set up, and the calendar on the wall, the moment that really let him know he could be at home in his new place was when he and my friend, father and son, settled in to watch Sixty Minutes. TV and/or radio can provide entertainment for all people, but especially for people who are no longer able to get out much. The world comes to them instead. Keeping those forms of communication working and easy for our loved ones to turn on and set up is very helpful. Such electronics also provide important companionship for the time spent alone.

*Helping my loved one have access to the outside world through TV or radio, through phone or internet, is a way to help expand their limited world.*

## *November 14*

***"What the world really needs is more love and less paperwork."***

—Pearl Bailey

This is so true, in a way that makes many of us smile at its irony. One can't escape the paperwork of life, but it is important always to remember that the love matters more. There were times when I was dismayed by how much paperwork there was for both of my parents—for their medical and other needs. For sure, any time that they moved locations, into a hospital or into a new facility, the paperwork was multiplied. I learned to know exactly where in their wallets were their Medicare cards, insurance cards, and other vital pieces of information.

Although we all agree with Pearl Bailey, it is helpful to have a sense of humor and acceptance about the need for paperwork. It is always best to just do it and not procrastinate. And then, get back to the more enjoyable task of loving.

*Part of loving is doing the paperwork, but the better part of loving is just getting back to being with each other.*

## *November 15*

***"You are a child of the universe. No less than the trees and the stars you have a right to be here. And whether or not it is clear to you, the universe is unfolding as it should."***

—Desiderata

More than once I found myself responding to a loved one—first my grandmother, then my father, and then my mother—as they expressed a puzzlement at still being alive, as they expressed being ready to leave this world. There is no easy response to this sentiment, and perhaps empathetic listening is the best we can offer. The timing of the universe can sometimes be hard to understand from our limited perspective.

We are all children of the universe. The words of this very old prayer remind all of us that we belong here until it is our time to leave this world. Until that time, we are each other's trees and stars. We take refuge in the light-giving breath of each other's leaves, and our love lights up the darkness as does the Milky Way's multitude of stars.

*Being here means we belong here—for ourselves as caregivers and for our loved ones. We each have a special part in a much larger whole.*

## *November 16*

***"One of the most important things you can do on this earth is to let people know they are not alone."***

—Shannon L. Alder

When we take time to contemplate our loved ones, we can probably step into the uncertainty they are feeling. Loss of health and loss of abilities one has known for a lifetime must be frightening, unsettling, and difficult to accept. As caregivers, we cannot change what is happening to our dear loved one. But we can let them know they are not alone, and this is a huge gift.

As caregivers, our listening ear in person or over the phone can make a difference that warms a day with the knowledge of companionship. Most of us human beings have known the ache of lonely days; our presence at a vulnerable time eases that ache for our loved one. Most days, there is no need for us to change or fix anything. Most days, just showing up in any way that we can reminds our loved one they are not alone. And this makes all the difference.

*Accompanying my loved one on this journey is one of the most important things I am doing at this time. As I ease their loneliness, I am also easing my own.*

## *November 17*

***"The blessing of nostalgia is that it can serve to remind us that just as we survived all of life before this . . . we can also live through this age with the same grace, the same insights . . . "***

—Joan Chittester

Moments of nostalgia nourish the part of us that forgets the richness of past times. Oddly, such nostalgia can also nourish the present. Nostalgia shared with a vulnerable loved one helps us both remember them in their prime. Perhaps you can remember a particular accomplishment in their life or a celebration of a life event that was a joyful gathering. Sometimes the memory of an adventurous trip taken in the past can be a touchstone to our loved one's inner strength. Even the memory of difficult times can remind us of fortitude and courage.

Photos are great for inspiring moments of nostalgia, but conversation is also a fruitful way to reminisce. Touchstones to the past bring up tender feelings but also help our loved one remember the full range of who they have been. All that life experience and wisdom lives inside of them, and nostalgia can be a bridge to remembering their inner strength.

*It is a blessing to remember with our loved one their lifelong strengths and accomplishments. Nostalgic moments imbue the present with awareness of that strength.*

## *November 18*

***"It was always the power of love that pulled us through. And it was always the power of laughter that kept us from falling apart."***

—Steve Rizzo

Love and laughter are a life-giving, alliterative combination. It is the power of love that pulls us through the challenging days: the hand that is held as bad news is delivered, the quiet companionship through days of ill health and pain. The quiet and amazing comfort of knowing we are loved or knowing we are loving a dear one through a very difficult time.

And yet, it is the sense of humor that also really helps one to manage. Perhaps it's the wry humor at life's absurdities and surprises, perhaps the humor of mistaken words or the day's bad joke. Always, laughter lightens the heart, and that lightening of the heart gives us the energy for a few more miles.

*Today let me honor my path of love and also of laughter; together, they make my days more lyrical—another alliteration.*

## *November 19*

***"Life, for all its agonies . . . is exciting and beautiful, amusing and artful and endearing . . . and whatever is to come after it—we shall not have this life again."***

—Rose Macauley

I know there are friends and family members who questioned some of my choices around caregiving as being more than what was necessary. What is important to me is that I gave it my all, given the limitations of my life at that time. Yes, there were times it was agonizing; accompanying a loved one through painful or sick days is not easy.

But there were many more moments that were endearing. There was an adventure to being so close to other beloved ones and my mom's experience as her life force waned; it was fascinating and often surprising. Unexpected gifts came my way. There was endless potential to be creative, to let beauty and art and humor transform us in so many little ways. That time in my life is now behind me; it truly doesn't last forever.

*Let me embrace fully this life I am living today;*
*I am ready to honor the adventure of being alive*
*and sharing this life with my loved one.*

## *November 20*

***" . . . I set out to stage the perfect holiday, for just me and my mother, in her nursing home room, a contradiction in terms if I ever heard one."***

—Jane Gross

If your loved one lives in your home, holidays might be more labor-intensive, but you have the gift of a home environment. For those whose loved ones live in facilities, even the most well-run and cheerful ones, those holidays can be tough. For everyone. No one wants to spend a holiday in a facility. But look around and you will find others, with quiet courage, making their best efforts for and with their loved one. You are not alone.

I remember a couple of Thanksgivings where several of my siblings showed up, where we pooled our potluck items. Strung special lights to make it look festive. "Ooh"-ed and "Aah"-ed over pie. It was much easier to stay in than to take our frail mother out, so we all made the best of it. It wasn't ideal, but we were together, trading stories, sharing some favorite memories of Thanksgivings of the past. And we carried on with the tradition of saying what we were grateful for—which all boiled down to being alive that day, together, and savoring traditional and favorite treats.

*Setting aside the myth of the perfect holiday,*
*I can focus on the gift of gathering together,*
*of life itself, and celebrating in simple ways.*

## *November 21*

***"To feel the love of people whom we love is a fire that feeds our life."***

—Pablo Neruda

Let's talk about what often doesn't get much attention on this journey—the love we receive as we share time with our beloved family member who is failing in some way. They are rarely failing in their ability to love; as the mind and body lose strength, the heart of love beats on. In a deep and true sense, it is this love that feeds our inner fire and keeps us going.

Love is the gift of this journey. The moments of gratitude from my loved ones in the midst of hard days have stayed with me years later. The memory of the smiles on their faces as I walked through the door reminds me today to light up as loved ones enter my door or my day.

*Caregiving provides me with an abundance of love; I will open my arms wide to it today.*

## November 22

**"Follow the grain in your own wood."**

—Howard Thurman

There is no defined path for the caregiver, which is part of its challenge. Each person's situation is a unique blend: perhaps our loved one has severe memory issues, perhaps our loved one is mentally alert but physically limited, perhaps our loved one lives inside of daily physical or emotional pain. There are many varieties of living situations, and they tend to change over time. There are all the variations in competence at such facilities.

And beyond all of those logistics, there are also unique stories of faith, belief, rituals, and ways of looking at the world we share with our loved one. So it is important to listen closely to our own needs and to those of our loved one and to trust our instincts. For me, this meant listening to the things that really mattered to my mom and doing what I could to make that accessible for her. Sometimes I needed to push for this in spite of a lack of enthusiasm from others around us. Always there was the reward of a happy, contented, or special experience for me and my loved one.

*That idea tugging at me, that beautiful grain*
*inside the wood, is worth following.*
*I can find creative ways to carve out*
*a loving path for my loved one.*

## *November 23*

***"You do not have to be perfect. You do not have to be an expert. All you need to do is care enough to try."***

—Kirsten DeLeo

It is easy to wonder if we are the best person for this job. Do we know enough? Understand the intricacies of the medical world enough? Do we have the emotional endurance to truly enter into this? Do we have the discernment to know what to say and do next? Are we strong enough to advocate for our loved one's needs?

But the caregiver is someone who has looked around and seen the need and felt a desire or calling to meet that need. The caregiver is most often motivated by love—usually for the loved one or perhaps for who the loved one was in their family constellation. Or, to help out another beloved family member. The initial impulse is to be a caring person for your loved one who is in need, and that will carry you all the way and teach as you go.

*There is no need for me to be the "perfect" person for this job. All that I need is my desire to care for and love this person through a difficult path. That will light my way.*

## *November 24*

***"What do we live for if it is not to make life less difficult for each other."***

—George Eliot

I have vivid memories of moments when we had to give our mother bad news. The death of a beloved nephew of hers, the divorce papers served to a young friend she truly cared about. My sister and I were careful about how and when we gave her the news; the most important thing was to do so at a time when we could be with her and not be rushed nor in need of heading off to another commitment.

Although we could do nothing to soften the news itself, what we could do was make it a little less difficult to receive by being with her, letting her ask the questions, and sharing the sadness. Sometimes she wanted to make a phone call or write a card in response, and then we could help her do so. There was a heightened sense of meaningfulness and usefulness to those days, which I felt then but appreciate also in hindsight.

*Let me appreciate the ways that being*
*a caregiver gives me the opportunity*
*to make life less difficult for my loved one—*
*it truly is an opportunity for gratitude.*

## *November 25*

***"Love and time—those are the only two things in all the world and all of life that cannot be bought but only spent."***

—Gary Jennings

Being a caregiver is like working on a graduate degree, the mission statement of which could be the above quote. Caregiving is all about the gift of love and time—two commodities that cannot be bought. Two concepts that live outside of our so often quantifiable and consumer-oriented society. This is one of the many hidden gifts of being a caregiver, for we enter a world where only time and love matter. We enter a world that is scaled down to the essence of what is most meaningful.

It is an opportunity to remember every day what is really important in life. And as easily distracted human beings, we tend to need reminders. When we enter that sacred space with our loved one—whether in person or by phone or through email or letters—we enter the realm that touches most deeply their and our spirits.

*Today I can be so grateful for how caregiving reminds me every day of the importance of the gifts of love and time, which don't cost anything.*

## *November 26*

***"The bluebird carries the sky on his back."***

—Henry David Thoreau

The bluebird is a tiny, incredibly beautiful shade-of-blue bird which rarely weighs more than an ounce and is known for roaming the countryside in small groups. It is a visual treat to see one in nature, and the backdrop is almost always an endless sky. The vision of the bird carrying the sky on its back upends how we might usually see both the sky and the bird.

The takeaway? The bird carries the sky on its back without realizing it does so. It flaps its wings, it travels with friends and family members, it moves lightly through the world. As caregivers, we can also move lightly through the backdrop of our burdens. We can even borrow from the bird's greatest asset—it sings easily and effortlessly as it moves through its days.

*Today I can sing and carry my burdens lightly. I can borrow from the energy and way of being of the beautiful and buoyant bluebird.*

## *November 27*

***"My heart, which is so full to overflowing, has often been solaced and refreshed by music when sick and weary."***

—Martin Luther

There are so many ways to bring music to the people we love. Music is something they can listen to when alone, on the days when no one can visit. Comforting chords can help make someone feel less alone, while other music will lift a person's spirit. One of my friend's fathers loves to listen to jazz. The mother of another friend, who has dementia, still loves to listen to musicals and often surprisingly remembers many of the lyrics. My own mother preferred hymns or Irish tunes and a few favorite musicals.

Music is also a balm for the caregiver. Often on my ride home, listening to calming, soothing, or upbeat music helped soften the hard edges of the day's challenges. There were drives when I needed thoughtful, beautifully sad music. And there were drives where an upbeat jazz tune was just what I needed.

*Music can bring solace to both my loved one and myself, and it is one of the many ways we can refresh ourselves.*

## *November 28*

***"Regardless of what challenge you are facing right now, know that it has not come to stay. It has come to pass. During these times, do what you can with what you have, and ask for help if needed."***

—Les Brown

Sometimes words allow us to look at something in a new way, through a special slant of light. The difference between come to stay and come to pass is only one word, and yet come to pass brings us into the concept of what is happening right now, unfolding in present time. There were moments when I was caregiving when I had that sensation that things were going to be this hard for a long time. Sometimes one day felt forever. If I could step back in time now, I would tell myself to cherish the moments in their passing. Now, they truly seem fleeting.

During difficult days, we need reminders to take it a day at a time or an hour at a time. We need reminders that doing the best we can is good enough, and we certainly need encouragement to reach out for help when we feel overwhelmed. Help is just one asking away.

*Today I will cherish what has come to pass and remind myself to fully appreciate what will, by definition, not stay forever.*

## *November 29*

***"The root of joy is gratefulness . . . It is not joy that makes us grateful; it is gratitude that makes us joyful."***

—Brother David Stendal-Rast

The other day, a friend of ours posted on YouTube how he celebrated almost 50 years of marriage with his wife who is in a facility for memory care, who he couldn't actually visit due to COVID-19. With the help of one of their children, two plates of a favorite meal were prepared, one for him on the outside and one for her on the inside. Each had a glass of sparkling water to raise to each other. He was dressed up in a tuxedo, their daughter and filmmaker played some of their favorite music, and through the glass they toasted their fifty years and celebrated.

There was such apparent joy in both of their faces. Gratitude for the many years together and a joy in still showing up for each other. Days later, the image stayed with me, for it was a stunning combination of love, courage, and creativity. It was a way of stepping over the dark days they had been through together to gratefully celebrate their shared decades of love.

*Celebrating important moments is an important opportunity to be grateful for all that we have shared.*

## *November 30*

***"Everybody needs beauty as well as bread, places to play in and pray in, where nature may heal and give strength to body and soul alike."***

—John Muir

I appreciate the reminder of the importance of both bread and beauty. Especially beauty. Food is essential, yes, so helping our loved ones eat well is important. But it is easy to forget the importance of beauty, especially natural beauty. Often a short trip out of doors, with my mother in a wheelchair (depending of course on the time of year), was something she deeply appreciated. The fresh air and the greenery of trees and bushes, even on that short path around her living facility, seemed to lift her spirits. In the fall, to be out among golden leaves was also a treat. On days she didn't feel good enough to go out, a small bouquet of whatever flower was in bloom brought the beauty of nature into her small living space.

My brother knew of her favorite yellow wildflower, and when it was in bloom, he always brought her a bouquet. This was so important and special for her. Another brother always brought her a small living pine tree for the holidays. One string of lights around its small circumference and its hint of a pine scent, and her place was transformed—from the ordinary into a powerful presence of color and a tangible presence of the natural world.

*I will keep my eyes and heart open for simple ways to bring the beauty of nature into my loved one's world. It is a timeless way to heal everyone's spirit.*

# December

## *December 1*

***"Music . . . can name the unnameable and communicate the unknowable."***

—Leonard Bernstein

There is a musical group in my city that is combined of family members and those who suffer from dementia or other kinds of memory loss. They sing together. Studies have shown that many people who have forgotten much still remember songs, both words and melodies. This is a wonderful way for them to be together, immersed in a common love of song.

Something unknowable and in some ways unnameable happens when music becomes the bridge to connect human hearts. Music takes over where words cannot go. Over the course of a lifetime, most of us have had many powerful experiences that were underscored by music. In the gentle days of caregiving, there are many ways we can bring music into the experience—to soothe our loved ones and ourselves. Listening to music, singing, or humming are all ways that mysteriously connect us to one another and to a life force of memory.

*Today I can let music be part of my caregiving; there are many ways to do so.*

## December 2

***"I still miss those I loved who are no longer with me but I find I am grateful for having loved them. The gratitude has finally conquered the loss."***

—Rita Mae Brown

"Grateful for having loved them" could describe many situations. But one of the true gifts of caregiving is that we have the opportunity to actively love someone through a difficult time. Whoever that person has been to us, whatever all the factors are that have informed our choice to take on this role, we can rest inside the circle of knowing we have made a choice to love in a concrete and caring way.

While our loved one is still living, we cannot fully grasp what our time giving care to them will mean. We are often so far inside of the situation, it is hard to reflect upon it. But this time shared with this loved one is such a gift; we can hone our sense of gratitude inside of each day. This gratitude is a solace against loss; you will be grateful for the rest of your life for the efforts of your caregiving. When the time was ripe, you were there.

*Gratitude for my time with my loved one is an overriding gift of this journey; such gratitude can carry me through this day and will shed a special light on this time as I carry it into the future.*

## *December 3*

***"Never lose sight of the fact that old age needs so little but needs that little so much."***

—Margaret Willour

Whether the person you are giving care to is aging or suffering from an illness, the above statement is so true. When one is vulnerable, needs both shrink and deepen. External needs such as acquiring things or achieving goals all become less important and perhaps completely fade away. The needs that remain are much more focused around being present to the day's needs and gifts.

When my parents were doing well, gifts to them ranged from tickets for shared events, to travel, to a shared purchase for an item they could use in their apartment. As they aged, material things mattered less and less. Ultimately what mattered the most was hearing from their loved ones and, better yet, visits from and with their loved ones.

*One of the basic and essential needs of all humans is to know we are cared about and for; this is especially true in vulnerable times. Today, my presence and my care match the transforming needs of my loved one.*

## *December 4*

***"When we investigate, we find beneath the grief of anger a reservoir of sadness. And beneath that sadness, an ocean of love beyond our wildest dreams."***

—Stephen Levine

In my caregiving days, I often felt like I was rushing. So much to do. So much to tend to. Sometimes the sheer weight of busyness or the particular challenges of any day laced a thread of anger through me. It wore a lot of different masks and pulled me in multiple directions. Feelings are always okay, I told myself, but they are also signs and symbols of deeper truths that are worthy of our attention.

When we slow down and investigate our anger, beneath it is often the grief of loss or of disappointed expectations. Sometimes it is easier to be angry than to be sad, but caring takes many forms. Sadness invites expression rather than lashing out, and sadness honored deepens and opens our hearts. Inside the opening pumps a deep well of love. If we didn't care so much, we couldn't be feeling this wide and deep array of emotions.

*Today I will honor the feelings I am wrestling*
*with for the core of what they are—*
*a deep and wild ocean of love.*
*To live fully is to love fully.*

## *December 5*

***"We all have an unsuspected reserve of strength inside that emerges when life puts us to the test."***

—Isabel Allende

Internationally known author Allende accompanied her daughter Paula through a grave illness, coma, and early death. It is such a difficult and heartbreaking path to care for and then lose a child. For each of us, as we tend to loved ones, there are particular challenges, and many of them are emotional. There were moments inside of my caregiving days when I wondered how I could keep going, how I could keep sustaining myself. And when I look back, I sometimes wonder how I balanced it all.

But in the moment, I do think we all have those reserves of strength. Gratefully, we can count on them to kick in when and as needed. It is helpful to trust that we have inside of us all that we need for this journey. Strength, the ability to ask for help, tools for rejuvenating ourselves, and reserves of strength. They will emerge as needed.

*Today I can trust that my reserves of strength will get me through each day. And I can ask for support from my team when my reserves need bolstering.*

## *December 6*

***"Sometimes it is necessary to reteach a thing its loveliness . . . until it flowers again from within . . . "***

—Galway Kinnell

There are abundant opportunities for both wilting and re-blooming along the mountainous path of caregiving. Sometimes the path is a narrow ledge with a steep drop-off. An intense focus is required to stay safely on the trail. Sometimes the path winds through uplifting meadows of wildflowers. Sometimes the wind tries to blow us off course. Other times the wind delivers sweet scents from surprising sources.

When times are tough, it's easy to feel discouraged, as a loved one in need and as a caregiver. But within each of us lies a powerful ability to flower, to bloom. I am always struck by flowers that emerge from the tiniest of cracks in rock or cement. The desire to blossom lies deep inside of all living things. It lies inside of us, ready to flower again and again, finding the opening through granite rock or volatile winds.

*When we are feeling wilted or uninspired,*
*we can reteach ourselves—or allow ourselves*
*to be retaught by loved ones around us—*
*our own particular loveliness.*
*Love is the center of that word and that ideal.*

## *December 7*

***"To care for those who once cared for us is one of the highest honors."***

—Tia Walker

One day I met my Muslim friend for coffee. She was telling me how in her religion and culture, caregivers are among the most respected. Kindness and love are prayerful values, and those who take care of the elderly, the sick, and the struggling ones are highly honored. In her family and community, her mother is widely known as a caregiver and is sought out often and deeply admired and respected for her caring nature.

What a beautiful sense of community and community values, I thought. So often in our results-focused culture, what is unseen or unquantifiable is often less valued. Value is so often tied to monetary gain. It helps me to know that there are communities, perhaps all around me, who highly value the unseen and unquantifiable work of caregivers. For inside my own experience, even in times of little external appreciation, I felt deeply the honor it was to be accompanying so closely my mother and father, also beloved aunts and uncle, as they walked toward the ends of their days. The time spent with them in their vulnerable moments still feels like sacred time, years later.

*It is an honor to be a caregiver to this special human being in my life. Even on days that my efforts don't feel wholly appreciated, I acknowledge this meaningful and intimate journey.*

## *December 8*

***"And it is still true, no matter how old you are, when you go out into the world it is best to hold hands and stick together."***

—Robert Fulghum

When I first saw Michelangelo's painting *The Creation of Adam* on the ceiling of the Sistine Chapel, I was all of about 22. I was a cynical questioner of every tradition I had ever known. But I will never forget how awed and moved I was by this amazing depiction of two hands touching. In this painting, it is the hand of God touching an earthly hand, Adam. In an incredible and artistic way, the image conveys the power of the touching of hands. In a different art form, in the famous movie ET, it is ET's long finger reaching out to touch human hands that is a prevailing image, especially as he says, "ET phone home . . . "

Hands connect us to one another and communicate comfort wordlessly. The touching of hands, the holding of hands is so simple and yet so powerful in its tenderness and its desire to bridge a gap between species or between two humans. One day, my Mom asked me to trim her nails, and that half hour spent holding her hands, finger by finger, is an enormously tender memory I will always hold close.

*Throughout my days of caregiving, let me remember the simple comfort of holding hands or touching hands with my loved one. It is a gesture in which the giving and receiving of care is embodied, both ways.*

## *December 9*

***"No matter what you've done for yourself or for humanity if you can't look back on having given love and attention to your own family what have you really accomplished?"***

—Lee Iacocca

The pulls of the world are many and often more glamorous than the role of caregiving. So often, the bottom line seems to be the paycheck or the prestige one is gaining or seeking in the world. And yet, we are bound to one another in ways that truly matter. And perhaps the true test of anyone's character is how they treat their close family and friends. And once an ailing or aging loved one is gone, we can only look back.

So in some ways, the caregiving we put our hearts into today is an investment in the future. Most of us want to know that we gave when it was needed and that we were there for those who had given much to us or to our families in previous and better years. To show up when a loved one is vulnerable is, in its own way, a deeply meaningful accomplishment.

*Today I will cherish my ability to care for a loved one and know that in a mysterious way, I am at the same time caring for myself.*

## *December 10*

***"Nature can bring you to stillness, that is its gift to you."***

—Eckhart Tolle

In my mother's assisted living facility, they used to set up an incubator every spring with baby chicken eggs. Under the glow lights, the eggs warmed and were watched closely by all the residents. Such excitement as those eggs hatched! As the babies emerged! Residents and visitors alike were fascinated. And when the fuzzy yellow beings emerged, we could all watch them learn to feed themselves, and of course grow. They were magical balls of yellow that could wobble on skinny short legs and cheep and chirp vibrant lullabies with each other.

I am convinced that time stood still for all of us as we observed this birthing of life before our eyes. It was such a gift that this facility brought this particular glimpse of nature to its residents. We watched eggs about to hatch, watched the cracking shell as they hatched, watched the yellow miracles emerge and then grow. All other concerns melted away as we, caregivers and care receivers alike, entered a timeless gift of nature. Birth. Life. Growth.

*Nature has abundant ways to bring me and*
*my loved one to a moment of stillness,*
*to the miracle of life that is now and today.*

## *December 11*

***"We can learn to rejoice in even the smallest blessings our life holds. It is easy to miss our own good fortune."***

—Pema Chodron

There is a mindful meditation that takes the meditator through appreciating each of his or her working body parts. Gratitude for eyes, ears, a mobile body, hands, feet, heartbeat, breath. When I do this, I am reminded how much I appreciate being healthy, especially right after I have been sick. Yet, how easily we forget to stay consciously grateful for health. This meditation is a way to consciously appreciate all that we have right now and today.

Beyond the miracle of a working body, there are many other things in each of our lives to be grateful for: loving friends or partner, other family members, the comforts of home, the presence of our loved one. In the rush to do all that needs doing, in the midst of the demands of a caregiver's life, a few moments of appreciation, yes even joy, for our blessings can help re-orient us to true north.

*I will take a few moments today to honor the blessings and good fortune that are a part of my life; these fuel what I have to give as a human being.*

## *December 12*

***"Spiritual energy brings compassion into the real world. With compassion, we see benevolently our own human condition and the condition of our fellow beings."***

—Christina Baldwin

We may have many different words or visions for it, yet most caregivers agree that this role, this job, touches and engages our spirits. It opens our eyes and hearts in compassionate ways. It gives us an opportunity to see up close our own basic needs and those of our loved one. To see those needs in a benevolent light is the challenge—the spiritual challenge.

Sometimes seeing ourselves in a benevolent light means being gentle with all the feelings coursing through our veins. Sometimes it means finding a way to nurture our hearts or heal our body aches. Seeing our loved one in a benevolent light can call us to a fuller presence or might inspire a kindness that is appropriate and special for this day.

*The spirit that feeds my source is helping me every day to see myself and my loved one through benevolent and caring eyes.*

## *December 13*

***"Grief can be the garden of compassion. If you keep your heart open through everything, your pain can become your greatest ally in your life's search for love and wisdom."***

—Rumi

Grief is an integral part of the journey of taking care of a failing or struggling loved one. You are witnessing a person who is transforming in a way that leaves behind their physical capabilities or diminishes other parts of who they used to be. Tears and sadness are a part of this journey. A musical parent who can no longer sing on key. A former athlete who now needs assistance to walk. A learned historian who can no longer remember yesterday.

And yet, the loved one is teaching you. As grief washes through you, what are you learning about the process of life and love? What quiet pieces of wisdom come to you through time shared with this person? What are you learning about them and about yourself at the same time? How does this time shape and deepen who you are for the rest of your life?

*The painful aspects of caregiving are often what lead me toward hard-earned wisdom and the deep empathy of an ever-opening heart. I may not feel it today, but I can believe in its presence.*

## *December 14*

***"Self-compassion is simply giving the same kindness to ourselves that we would give to others."***

—Christopher Germer

The gymnast on the balance beam finds her way in spite of pulls to both edges of the narrow beam. Caregivers walk a thinly veiled line between caring for others and self-care. It is never an even equation. But we can see people who bend too far one way or another. The caregiver who becomes sicker than the loved one she was caring for is not all that uncommon.

The challenge of the caregiver is to balance kindnesses that reach out into the world with kindness to ourselves. Some of us may be able to create regular rituals of self-kindness: a weekly walk with a friend, a commitment to a caregivers support group. Such regular support and care of ourselves can be enormously helpful to keep us going. Sometimes we may realize how worn out we are and need to declare a day or weekend of self-nurturing. For those who live with their loved one, time for oneself can be very difficult to find. One such person told me it helped her to list what she was grateful for—that tangible list always gave her hope and a wider lens to joy.

*On this journey as a caregiver, it is essential that I remember to be kind to myself and honor the ways I need to be refueled.*

## *December 15*

***"The moment one gives close attention to anything, even a blade of grass, it becomes a mysterious, awesome, indescribably magnificent world in itself."***

—Henry Miller

I was remembering the other day about my maternal grandmother, how she hosted coffee time in her very tiny apartment every afternoon at 4:00. Her two daughters who both lived nearby—my mother and my aunt—came most days. But so did we grandchildren, which gave my mom or aunt a day off. When I was in high school, I was too busy or too cool for this, but after I left home for college, I cherished this special time with her. When I came home on breaks, I often planned my day around this 4:00 ritual. She always had a cookie jar full of fresh cookies, and in fact, she baked right up until the day she died.

Forty years later, I remember the sweetness of this simple ritual and the happiness in my grandmother's eyes when we gathered around her. News of the day was often simple; it was just being together that really mattered. I was thinking of this the other day and missing her, and then missing my mother, who I wanted to call in that moment to remember all the different kinds of cookies we enjoyed there.

*Moments shared can fool us in their simplicity.*
*Attention makes the imprint that is not*
*lost over time. Let me give my attention*
*to the love around me today.*

## *December 16*

***"People think angels fly because they have wings. Angels fly because they take themselves lightly."***

—Source unknown

I appreciate the message of this quote not because I think we should aspire to being angels but because I love the imagery of lightness and flight. Taking oneself lightly means to approach the world in a lighthearted way, to find ways to carry our burdens without letting them weigh us down. To take oneself lightly means to laugh easily.

These are all great reminders as we move through the often difficult days of caregiving. Perhaps there is one aide at the facility who always cheers us up. Perhaps we have one friend who helps put a humorous spin on anything. Perhaps there is that private joke we have going with our loved one or with someone on our caregiving team. In these ways, we invite lightness and lightheartedness into our days. Angelic flight is not necessarily within our reach, but a lighter step and an easier laugh can carry us a long way.

*Today I will look for ways to take myself and my day as a caregiver lightly.*

## *December 17*

***"Gently, she laughs***
***With . . . brilliant inquisitiveness, and that same ancient confusion that is deep within the soul of every beautiful living being."***

—Ray Quesada, *"But She is a Caring Soul"*

The combination of laughter and confusion is striking in this quote as well as how both qualities are connected to an ancient tradition among beautiful living beings and their souls. The term "ancient confusion" captures that sense which many of us feel, at least from time to time. The phrase "what's it all about" speaks to this larger-than-life, existential question. Amid the many details that are part of caregiving, alongside the deep quality-of-life questions being lived, there is ample opportunity for ancient confusion.

Laughter always eases fear and anxiety. A simple shared and good-humored response to life's absurdity can help lighten a heavy moment. Humor can come in many forms, and often the gentle and subtle moments of humor can be the most transformative. Life does have its absurd and surprising and sometimes almost unbelievable twists and turns. Shaking our heads in ancient confusion, we may as well celebrate when we can with gentle humor.

*Part of being a beautiful soul in this world is acknowledging our ancient confusion—there is no road map for this journey.*

## *December 18*

***"Whatever you are doing, love yourself for doing it. Whatever you are feeling, love yourself for feeling it."***

—Thaddeus Golas

There is a lot to be said for fully embracing the journey of caregiver. I sometimes think of it as having a Tolkien-like adventure quality. Only instead of being out in the forest with giants and eerie creatures seeking to do us harm, the journey is in the details. It's in the valleys of disappointment and the long climbs uphill to keep our loved one nourished and nurtured. The adventure is imbued with meaning as we honor the many emotional dips and rises.

The journey is also in the moments of sunshine breaking through clouds. It's in the moments of taking a break together and breathing, sharing food, drink, and the view together. It's in the moments when life's absurdity brings on shared laughter. We are like pilgrims as we enter the forest of each day, as we take on obstacles and winding paths. Rather than seeing the journey as a well-worn trail, we can honor its true depths and heights by fully loving what we are doing and by fully embracing the wide range of feelings we encounter.

*Today I can simply remember to honor and love this journey.*

## *December 19*

***"Change always involves a dark night when everything falls apart. Yet if this period of dissolution is used to create new meaning, then chaos ends and new order emerges."***

—Margaret Wheatley

When I was buying adult diapers for my father, I had a breakdown. It was a new level of dependence for him. When my mother could no longer get in and out of our cars, our world shrank a bit. When my neighbor's forgetful mother went out for a walk and got lost, they knew she needed a memory care unit. There any many small changes along this road and some big ones, and they all require an adjustment. It feels like things are falling apart, and yes, in some way they are. The shifts can feel seismic.

Yet, there is potential to move into a newly meaningful truth. My parents were inching their way to the end. My neighbor's mother is much safer where she is, and this brings relief for my neighbor. Out of chaos, new order. It is often hard fought for, but the new sense of meaning is always within reach.

*If I am in the middle of a dark night,*
*I can trust that a clearer sense*
*of meaning will emerge for all of us.*

## *December 20*

***"I have all the courage I need; the more I use, the more I have."***

—Jean Illsley Clark and Connie Dawson

Advocating or speaking up is not necessarily my strong suit. Yet, there were definitely times when I needed to speak up to advocate for better care for one of my parents, to address an issue with a sibling, or to ask for the kind of support I needed. All of these could feel hard, especially if I was feeling tired or run down from balancing caregiving and other parts of my busy life.

It takes both clarity and then courage to speak up for one's self or for one's loved one. Yet, courage does feed itself. Every time we step up in a time of need, we discover not only that we can do so but also that it is an effective way to achieve a better situation. It's always worth it to encourage ourselves to act where we see the need.

*Today I will trust that I have the courage to face the task at hand. After all, it is said that courage is fear that has said its prayers.*

## *December 21*

***"What is life? It is the flash of a firefly in the night. It is the breath of a buffalo in the wintertime. It is the little shadow which runs across the grass and loses itself in the sunset."***

—Crowfoot

Life is fleeting. Time flies. Don't blink or you will miss it. There are many sayings about how quickly the days slip through our hands or rather, the hands of time. When one thinks of a lifetime or of eternity, we can see how short this particular phase of life is. If we have raised children, we might reflect upon how long ago the baby or the learning-to-walk-and-talk phases were. Many images have most likely flown by since then.

Our caregiving role may last a very long time, but it will not last forever. And when it is over, we will miss it—especially the presence of our loved one. It is helpful to remember that this time of life is particularly precious. Like the flash of a firefly in the night, it has a magical way of surprising us with its moments of illumination.

*Part of honoring today is knowing this special time with my loved one won't last forever.*

## *December 22*

***"No voice is too soft when that voice speaks for others."***

—Janna Cachola

If you are one of the many whose loved one lives in a facility, you know firsthand how there are many kind and competent workers there. And then there are the weaker, less competent ones. Few systems are set up to help those who are less effective, and that is why part of almost every caregiver's role is to advocate for the needs of our loved ones. Often it comes down to clearly communicating what our expectations are, what we see as essential needs for our loved one. It also means listening to and understanding the roles of those working with our loved one.

This requires clarity, patience, and diplomacy. Caring itself requires a lot of energy, so sometimes we want to put off advocating or do so in an irritated and ineffective way. We can gather the kindling in our hearts, which is clarity, even if it's just about what our questions are. Clarity is like kindling in that it feeds the flame of our energy and intention. As we speak up and advocate, we so often find there is a way to make things better.

*The spark of advocacy is an important part of my role; speaking up can help illuminate how to better understand and facilitate help where it is needed.*

## *December 23*

***"We are the living links in a life force that moves and plays through and around us, binding the deepest soils with the farthest stars."***

—Alan Chadwick

Caregiving is an important link in the chain of humanity. As many of us know all too well, there are gaps in the medical system, gaps in the way our culture cares for the vulnerable ones, and gaping holes in our ability to prepare for so many unforeseen challenges. The enormous number of caregivers in our country speaks to the vast need to make connections in place of those gaps.

We are links between generations, links between our loved ones' past and future. We are links connecting that which might be broken without our presence. We are conduits for a life force, and even though we might not be aware on a daily basis, we can take moments here and there to realize we are as much a part of the ongoing life force as the earth beneath us and the stars overhead.

*Like the earth beneath my feet and the stars*
*splashing light across the sky,*
*I am part of a huge life force,*
*and my role as a caregiver*
*is an important link.*

## *December 24*

***"The closest thing to being cared for is to care for someone else."***

—Carson McCullers

There is a kind of mysterious linkage that happens when one is caring for a loved one. There is an intimacy there that defies description but which has the potential almost daily to warm one's heart, whether one is the giver or receiver of care. Physicists would say that all of life is a form of energy and that relationships of all kinds are about an exchange of energy. So the exchange of energy in a caregiving situation is often a very rich one, layered with history and depths of meaning.

Admittedly, some days one can feel drained from caregiving; there are many good reasons for this. But also, one is in a very deep way caring for oneself as we care for others. It's almost inexplicable unless and until you experience it yourself. Love is an exchange of energy; it is dynamic.

*Today I will honor how I am caring for myself*
*as I care for my loved one. Love is love is love,*
*and love opens my heart and*
*lets the world in in surprising ways.*

## December 25

***"Nobody wants to hear about your nursing home holiday, no matter how sprightly the telling. No gift of gab is sufficient to turn one of life's black moments into a cocktail party story."***

—Jane Gross

I appreciate the sense of dark humor in this line. The journey from the old days of a long table, beautifully decorated, filled with family members and my parents, still doing well, presiding over the festivities to the holiday in a special room at the assisted living place is like crossing a suspension bridge with a steep drop beneath it. Two different worlds; very different eras. All over the world, such adjustments are being made. Traditions change based on the situation of the participants.

We made the best of it. Made it as festive as we could with special decorations and lights. Cherished the time together. One holiday, I organized a sing-along for my mom and the other residents. The music drew some people who rarely socialized, and my mom deeply appreciated that. The shared singing lifted everyone's spirits. Instead of singing around a beautifully decorated living room, we were singing in the community room, the lack of cozy décor being offset hugely by the voices joined in song, even if a little off-key!

*There is probably no way to adequately describe<br>the holidays' adaptation for my loved one.<br>But I and those closest to us understand.<br>And all over the world, I appreciate the<br>quiet courage of carrying on an old<br>tradition in a new and simpler way.*

## *December 26*

***"Real care of the sick does not begin with costly procedures but with the simple gift of affection and love . . . A kind heart is as valuable as medical training, because it is the source of happiness for both oneself and others."***

—The Dalai Lama

When I look up definitions or synonyms for kindness, the following words emerge: friendly, generous, considerate, tender, warm-hearted. This was the way I most wanted to show up for my loved one. But some days, that was hard. Some days, the frazzle and sense of overwhelm and ragged edges of resentment got to me. What often helped was to pause before I opened the door and take a few deep breaths. Consciously drop the frazzle, as if leaving it in a suitcase outside the door.

And truly, leaving that suitcase full of frazzle outside the door was the best thing I could do for her and for me. I was free then for the next amount of time (hour, an afternoon), to just be with her. To practice generosity, consideration. To slow down enough to feel tenderness for her and for me, for this time together. All the other concerns could, and would, wait.

*Real care matters. I immerse myself in real care when I show up with concern and consideration and leave behind, at least for a time, my other worries.*

## December 27

**"God gave burdens; he (she, they) also gave shoulders."**

—Yiddish Proverb

An often repeated saying is that we are never given more than we can handle. I sometimes struggle with this saying because at times it seems to me people are given way too much to handle at one time. I have had to outgrow my ideas of fairness; life is more random than fair. The idea that we are also given shoulders to carry our burdens is helpful. Shoulders become a metaphor for all the ways in which we humans do carry what is difficult.

Inside the God-given and hard-earned toolbox are numerous ways to help us shoulder our burdens. They include muscles of love, the ability to reach out to others when we need help, creativity for ways to keep our loved one and ourselves engaged, a deep belief in the worth of our chosen path, energy that is fueled by compassion, and more. We may be carrying a lot right now, but we also have the strength and shoulders to balance the load and ourselves.

*When I feel burdened, I will remind myself*
*to look at all the tools I have to help*
*me lift and carry the burden.*
*Gratitude and creativity can replace weariness.*

## *December 28*

***"Kwanzaa affirms that mothers and fathers of previous generations transmitted African Americans' existence and persistence to the mothers and fathers of today. Pass it on."***

—Dorothy Winbush Riley

In the last days of December, African Americans celebrate the holiday of Kwanzaa. Candles are lit to celebrate the seven principles of Kwanzaa which utilize Kiswahili words: unity (umoja), self-determination (kujichagulia), collective work and responsibility (ujima), cooperative economics (ujamaa), purpose (nia), creativity (kuumba), and faith (imani). In that time before the ending of a year and the beginning of a new one, no matter our own ethnicity, we can pay attention to these principles in our own lives.

Existence and persistence are legacies to be celebrated and passed on. Rituals, sharing of food and gifts—these are all aspects of Kwanzaa. It is a powerful time of year for honoring what previous generations have contributed and for coming together to create a stronger sense of community. How might all of us spend some special time with our loved one thinking of one or more of these principles—such as faith or purpose or unity.

*When we strengthen our sense of community,*
*we embolden our hopes for the future.*

## *December 29*

***"Be comfortable when the conversation grows silent, and sit and enjoy each other's company. This can be incredibly meaningful and healing."***

—Kirsten DeLeo

So often we carry expectations for conversation, for cheering up our loved one. Yet, in truth, we don't need to provide anything in particular, except a holding of whatever mood or frame of mind our loved one is in. I often found it helpful to do a brief visualization before I opened the door to my mom's place: let go of expectations, let go of my other worries, to open my heart as I opened the door.

I truly think the smile or warm hello from anyone who entered my mom's room made a big difference for her. Sometimes, as we settled in for a cup of tea after I did a few small chores for her, the quiet would descend. I learned to listen for the peacefulness of those moments. I learned to just enjoy being in her presence. I was at some level aware that these were measured days, and thus, precious.

*Today, let me find the meaning in quiet simple moments shared with my loved one.*

## *December 30*

***"The winds of grace blow all the time. All we need to do is set our sails."***

—Ramakrishna

When a day feels hard, I sometimes ask for grace. Just the other day, with that feeling of molasses in my bones, of each step demanding so much of me, I asked for grace to get through the day. I put it out to the universe, then I began to take my steps into my day. An hour later, a blue heron flew over my head. I stopped and watched. Such gracefulness in its wide and generous wings, its slow unhurried flapping that lifted it up with utter smoothness and lowered it back to the water's edge with the same fluid motion.

Then an old friend called and shared with me a dilemma with her daughter because she knew I would understand. She is someone I truly admire, and I felt honored. One day, my mother looked at me and told me she loved to talk to me because I was a good listener. Another day, with tears in her eyes, she overflowed with thanks and gratitude for my and my siblings' ongoing presence in her days.

*Moments of grace are in the air all the time; some days we are better at sailing into them than others. Asking and looking for grace in our day often opens the way.*

## *December 31*

***"If the only prayer you said in your whole life was, 'thank you', that would suffice."***

—Meister Eckhart

There are a lot of reminders in the world around us of the importance of gratitude. There are even studies on how a practice of gratitude can impact our brain chemistry in healing and positive ways. As caregivers, we certainly have our days of feeling we have hardships to complain about. But it is extremely beneficial to remember on a daily basis the many gifts for which we are grateful. On a day when joy feels distant, a list of what we are grateful for provides a tangible touchstone to its quiet presence.

There is the gift of life; each day we awaken, we are lucky to have the gift of breath, of eyesight, of hearing, of movement, of health. And we are blessed to have our loved one in our lives. We are blessed to have a sense of purpose. We are blessed to share this day, each day, with all of our loved ones.

*On my busy and demanding caregiving path,*
*let me take time every day to be thankful*
*for the many gifts in my life.*

# *Resources*

## Reading resources helpful for caregivers:

Jane Brody, *A Bittersweet Season: Caring for Our Aging Parents and Ourselves.* (Vintage Books, 2012)
Atul Gawande, *Being Mortal: Medicine and What Matters in the End* (Metropolitan Books, 2014)
Caroline Johnson, *The Caregiver* (Holy Cow! Press, 2018)
Tove Pettersen, *Conceptions of Care: Altruism, Feminism, and Mature Care* (An Article from *Hypatia: A Journal of Feminist Philosophy*, 2012)
Barry J. Jacobs and Julia L. Mayer, *Meditations for Caregivers* (DeCapo Press/AARP, 2016)
Brene Brown, *The Power of Vulnerability* (Audio Book by Sounds True, 2012)
Brene Brown, *The Gifts of Imperfection* (Hazelden Publishing, 2010)
Kirsten DeLeo, *Present Through the End–A Caring Companion's Guide for Accompanying the Dying* (Shambhala Publications, 2019)
Richard Wagamese, *Embers: One Ojibway's Meditations* (Douglas and McIntyre Ltd., 2016)

## Other Resources:

### Regional

Senior Linkage
www.seniorlinkageline.com
800-333-2433

Wilder Foundation
St. Paul, MN
caregiving@wilder.org
651-280-2273

Family Caregivers Center of Mercy
Cedar Rapids Iowa
www.mercycare.org

### National

National Family Caregiver Support Program
https://www.acl.gov/programs/support-caregivers/national-family-caregiver-support-program

Resources and Support for Family Caregivers - AARP
www.aarp.org › caregiving

## *Copyright Credits*

## *About the Author*

Photo by Judy Griesedieck

Patricia Hoolihan's previous books include three daily meditation books: one for parents of teens, one for teen girls and one for mothers in recovery. She has also authored a book on parenting teens into adulthood and, most recently, published a memoir *Storm Prayers: Retrieving and Reimagining Matters of the Soul* (North Star Press). This book for caregivers is the one she wishes she had had when she was walking with her parents and other beloved family elders through their last months and years. She teaches writing at The Loft in Minneapolis and at Metropolitan State University.

For more information,
please visit www.patriciahoolihan.com.